World Crisis Foretold

How it began
What is ahead

What is needed
to meet it

ShelterRock
EXODUS 33:22
Books

HB–902
World Crisis Foretold
by E.G. White (chapters 1-5, 7-8)
     ShelterRock Editor (chapter 6)
Published by ShelterRock Books, Inc
Altamont, TN 37301 USA
Printed in the United States of America
Cover and Text Copyright © 2002

About the cover: We sorrow over the terrible tragedy that occurred in New York City on September 11, 2001. At 9:03 a.m., 17 minutes after the earlier impact, a second Boeing 767 was turned into a flying jet-fuel bomb. United Airlines Flight 175, hijacked en route from Boston to Los Angeles with 65 passengers aboard, struck floors 80 to 86 of the 110 story, 1,362-foot South World Trade Center. Fifty-seven minutes later, the first of the two towers collapsed. The other followed shortly afterward.

As we find ourselves a nation in defense against those who would seek to destroy us, will our liberties remain high, or will we sacrifice them in order to provide ourselves with greater security?

Sources of this book:

Everything in this book, with the exception of chapter 6, was written by E.G. White.

Chapters 1-5 are a condensation of the most crucial points in the book, *Great Controversy*, in the author's own words. (A more detailed source list will be found on page 125.) The subject matter is remarkably comprehensive.

Chapter 6 is a condensation of basic points in the book, *Beyond Pitcairn*.

Chapter 7 is a condensation of the book, *Steps to Christ*, in the author's own words.

Chapter 8 is a summary of basic health principles (by the author of chapters 1-5 and 7) in the author's own words.

Additional copies: For additional copies of this book at extremely low prices in boxful quantities, write to Shelter Rock, Altamont, TN 37301. When you write, ask for a copy of our "Missionary Book Order Sheet," containing low-cost boxful prices of this book and other books, such as Great Controversy, Ministry of Healing, Christ's Object Lessons, Bible Readings, the Conflict Series, etc.

Contents

Introduction

Events Today

— Foretold as much as 100 Years Ago

"Since 1945, it began to be technologically feasible to end life on this planet."—*Michael Grosso, "Analyzing the Future," in Isaac Asimov, ed., Living in the Future (1985), p. 18.*

Why did we seek to uncover that last, that deepest, secret? But now it is done and we stand aghast at what crazed men can now do to the rest of us.

"Man has survived, thitherto, through ignorance. Can he continue to survive now that the useful degree of ignorance is lost?"—*Bertrand Russell, Has Man a Future? historian and philosopher (1961), p. 69.*

Then came the 43-year nuclear arms race between the United States and the Soviet Union. For decades, there was a massive bipolar face-off between the Soviet Union and America; and the rest of the world quietly sat back and nervously watched.

But then, when the Soviet Union broke apart in 1989, everything changed again. Over a dozen smaller nations began preparing for war against one another—or against us.

In the 1990s, nations once again were arming,— but this time it is different. We have now entered upon a situation that has steadily grown almost unmanageable.

Now there are too many actors in the drama, too many loose nukes, too many individual terrorists. It is too easy to buy nuclear bombs, too easy to make chemical and biological ones.

The leading scientists and intelligence experts of America tell us they long for the days of the cold war, when things were peaceful!

"In comparison to the present, in some ways it seems like the Cold War was a piece of cake."—*National Security Seminar, late 1990s, held at the U.S. Army War College, Carlisle, Pennsylvania.*

Make no mistake: The 1990s and beyond have hurled us into an increasingly dangerous world. **The entire world is becoming increasingly militarized, and many of the belligerents are fanatics.**

We now live on the edge of a sudden military attack which could destroy major cities,—*an attack which need not come from the skies*. It can be brought in on trucks. **Yet there are a number of other,** *equally dangerous* **problems.** This is the story of what we are facing. Why it will come. And what you need to do to prepare for it.

Nuclear attack: **All the terrorists and rogue nations need is the raw material—the uranium or plutonium.** Once they have that, they can build the bombs. The underpaid workers at Russian storage sites are glad to secretly sell quantities of it. Bribery and black market selling have been standard market procedures in Russia for decades.

Writing in a 1997 intelligence digest, a nuclear weapons expert, Graham Allison, described the situation: Once fissionable material is obtainable, it can easily be made into weapons. **Transportation of the material is not difficult. A simple bomb design can be made with less than 20 pounds of plutonium.**

It would be easy to sneak such a bomb into America or another Western nation. Many rogue groups want the nuclear material and are willing to pay a lot to get it *(Graham T. Allison, "The Number One Threat of Nuclear Proliferation Today: Loose Nukes from Russia," The Brown Journal of World Affairs, Winter/Spring 1997, p. 65).*

Rarely mentioned by officials, but **a very serious "weapon," would be the small airplanes** parked at thousands of private airports in America. It would be easy to load explosives into a small plane, fill it with fuel, and fly it into government buildings. The combination of explosives and aviation fuel would be terrible. Jetliners are also not adequately protected. America is not guarding its airplanes!

The worst scenario, next to nuclear bombs, includes chemical and biological weapons:

Chemical weapons: The raw materials are relatively easy to get, and the finished products do not have to be kept alive. But, unlike germs, the chemicals cannot reproduce. So they can affect only a small area—unless a crop-dusting plane is used, which could cover a large city.

Only **a large terrorist syndicate could make tons of chemical weapons.** But it is known that Iraq has stockpiles of them. The 1995 Tokyo subway attack used a chemical weapon (sarin gas). Because an extremely small amount was used, few people died.

Biological weapons: Most feared are anthrax (a bacterium) and smallpox (a virus). Both are highly lethal. Inhalant anthrax kills nearly 90% of its victims; but anthrax is not communicable.

Smallpox kills about 30%, but can be transmitted with horrifying ease. **Experts believe smallpox is the worst of the two.**

Anthrax is turned into a weapon merely by releasing airborne spores for people to breathe. A plane flying over New York City could easily do it. Within a few days cold-like symptoms develop. **By the time the symptoms are noted, treatment is too late.** Death follows within a week.

Bubonic plague is the third major "weapons-grade" disease. Russian defectors have declared that, before its collapse, the Soviet Union was developing new super plagues (primarily strains of anthrax and smallpox which were more lethal), against which there would be no known antidotes. Following that collapse, it became far easier for foreign agents to bribe guards to sell them quantities of it.

Today 17 nations are believed to have biological weapons programs, many of which involve anthrax.

The ABOVE STATEMENT was written prior to September 11, 2001. (See our book, Beginning of the End.) If anything, the situation is now even more dangerous. We are hurtling toward oblivion. Only God can help us; yet, by our immoralities, we are declaring that we do not want His help.

We join the rest of America and the world in deep sorrow over the recent tragedies in New York City and Washington, D.C., which took the lives of thousands of innocent people. Our heartfelt prayers go out to the many who have suffered loss in these tragedies as well as in the ongoing battle against worldwide terrorism.

We are stunned as we consider that a terrible climax is now developing before our eyes, events leading to the destruction of this world. Yet, according to Bible prophecy, God is permitting this to happen. He often allows developments to work toward a climax, just as they have in the past. He did it in Noah's day, when He sent a flood of waters that buried the wicked. He did it in the days of Abraham, when He destroyed the cities of Sodom and Gomorrah because of their wickedness. When wickedness reaches a certain point, God steps in.

Christ predicted that, when conditions in the entire world became as evil as they were in the time of Noah and Sodom— the end would come!

Have we reached that point? Are the worldwide calamities a sign that we have reached the end?

Almost one hundred years ago the primary author of this book, E.G. White, was shown in vision what was to happen to the great cities of this world. Here are a few examples:

"Satan is exercising his power. He sweeps away the ripening harvest, and famine and distress follow. He imparts to the air a deadly taint, and thousands perish by the pestilence. These visitations are to become more and more frequent and disastrous."— *EGW, Great Controversy, 590.*

"On one occasion, when in New York City, I was in the night season called upon to behold buildings rising story after story toward heaven . . The scene that next passed before me was an alarm of fire. Men looked at the lofty and supposedly fireproof buildings and said: 'They are perfectly safe.' But these buildings were consumed as if made of pitch. The fire engines could do nothing to stay the destruction. The firemen were unable to operate the engines."—*EGW, 9 Testimonies, 12-13 (1909).*

"In the night I was, I thought, in a room but not in my own house. I was in a city, where I knew not, and I heard explosion after explosion. I rose up quickly in bed, and saw from my window large balls of fire. Jetting out were sparks, in the form of arrows, and buildings were being consumed, and in a very few minutes the entire block of buildings was falling and the screeching and mournful groans came distinctly to my ears. I cried out, in my raised position, to learn what was happening: Where am I? And where are our family circle? Then I awoke."—*EGW, Manuscript 126 (1906).*

"During a vision of the night, I stood on an eminence, from which I could see houses shaken like a reed in the wind. Buildings, great and small, were falling to the ground. Pleasure resorts, theaters, hotels, and the homes of the wealthy were shaken and shattered. Many lives were blotted out of existence, and the air was filled with the shrieks of the injured and the terrified . . One touch, and buildings, so thoroughly constructed that men regarded them as secure against every danger, quickly became heaps of rubbish. There was no assurance of safety in any place."—*EGW, 9 Testimonies, 92-93 (1909).*

"The crisis is stealing gradually upon us. The sun shines in the heavens, passing over its usual round, and the heavens still declare the glory of God. Men are still eating and drinking, planting and building, marrying and giving in marriage. Merchants are still buying and selling. Men are jostling one against another, contending for the highest place. Pleasure lovers are still crowding to theaters, horse races, gambling hells. The highest excitement prevails, yet probation's hour is fast closing, and every case is about to be eternally decided. Satan sees that his time is short. He has set all his agencies at work that men may be deceived, deluded, occupied, and entranced until the day of probation shall be ended, and the door of mercy forever shut."—*EGW, Southern Watchman, Oct. 3, 1905.*

Chapter One

Bringing a Planet into Rebellion

— Crisis of the Ages

How DID evil begin? Why IS there sin anyway? Here is one of the most sweeping chapters in this entire book of the ages. Read that most amazing of stories—how sin began —

Although surrounded by continual selflessness, something happened. What could turn an angel of light into a devil—and do it right in the middle of heaven? This is something you will want to read. It will tell you why God had to wait—and the wonderful future in store for His children—because He did —

Before the entrance of evil, there was peace and joy throughout the universe. All was in perfect harmony with the Creator's will. Love for God was supreme, love for one another impartial. Christ the Word, the only begotten of God, was one with the eternal Father,— one in nature, in character, and in purpose,—the only being in all the universe that could enter into all the counsels and purposes of God. By Christ, the Father wrought in the creation of all heavenly beings. "By Him were all things created, that are in Heaven . . whether they be thrones, or dominions, or principalities, or powers" (Col. 1:16); and to Christ, equally with the Father, all Heaven gave allegiance.

The law of love being the foundation of the government of God, the happiness of all created beings depended upon their perfect accord with its great principles of righteousness. God desires from all His creatures the service of love,—homage that springs from an intelligent appreciation of His character. **He takes no pleasure in a forced allegiance**, and to all He grants freedom of will that they may render Him voluntary service.

How Sin Began

But there was one that chose to pervert this freedom. **Sin originated with him who, next to Christ, had been most honored of God** and who stood highest in power and glory among the inhabitants of Heaven. **Before his fall, Lucifer was first of the covering cherubs, holy and undefiled.** "Thus saith the Lord God: Thou sealest up the sum, full of wisdom, and perfect in beauty. Thou hast been in Eden the garden of God; every precious stone was thy covering." "Thou art the anointed cherub that covereth; and I have set thee so; thou wast upon the holy mountain of God; thou hast walked up and down in the midst of the stones of fire. Thou wast perfect in thy way from the day that thou wast created, till iniquity was found in thee." *Ezekiel 28:12-15*.

Lucifer might have remained in favor with God, beloved and honored by all the angelic host, exercising his noble powers to bless others and to glorify His Maker. But, says the prophet, "Thine heart was lifted up because of thy beauty, thou hast corrupted thy wisdom by reason of thy brightness" (Eze. 28:17). **Little by little, Lucifer came to indulge a desire for self-exaltation.** "Thou hast set thine heart as the heart of God." "Thou hast said . . I will exalt my throne above the stars of God; I will sit also upon the mount of the congregation." "I will ascend above the heights of the clouds; I will be like the Most High." *Ezekiel 28:6; Isaiah 14:13-14*. **Instead of seeking to make God supreme in the affections and allegiance of His creatures, it was Lucifer's endeavor to win their service and homage to himself.** And, coveting the honor which the infinite Father had bestowed upon His Son, this prince of angels aspired to power which it was the prerogative of Christ alone to wield.

They Pleaded with Him

All Heaven had rejoiced to reflect the Creator's glory and to show forth His praise. And while God was thus honored, all had been peace and gladness. But a note of discord now marred the celestial harmonies. The service and exaltation of self, contrary to the Creator's plan, awakened forebodings of evil in minds to whom God's glory was supreme. **The heavenly councils pleaded with Lucifer.** The Son of God presented before him the greatness, the goodness, and the justice of the Creator, and the sacred, unchanging nature of His law. God Himself had established the order of Heaven; and in departing from it, Lucifer would dishonor his Maker and bring ruin upon himself. **But the warning, given in infinite love and mercy, only aroused a spirit of resistance. Lucifer allowed jealousy of Christ to prevail, and he became the more determined.**

Pride in his own glory nourished the desire for supremacy. The high honors conferred upon Lucifer were not appreciated as the gift of God, and called forth no gratitude to the Creator. He gloried in his brightness and exaltation, and aspired to be equal with God. He was beloved and reverenced by the heavenly host. Angels delighted to execute his commands, and he was clothed with wisdom and glory above them all. **Yet the Son of God was the acknowledged sovereign of Heaven, one in power and authority with the Father. In all the counsels of God, Christ was a participant while Lucifer was not permitted thus to enter into the divine purposes.** "Why," questioned this mighty angel, "should Christ have the supremacy? Why is He thus honored above Lucifer?"

Opposed to the Law of God

Leaving his place in the immediate presence of God, Lucifer went forth to diffuse the spirit of discontent among the angels. Working with mysterious secrecy, and for a time concealing his real purpose under an appearance of reverence for God, **he endeavored to excite dissatisfaction concerning the laws that governed**

heavenly beings, intimating that they imposed an un-necessary restraint. Since their natures were holy, he urged that the angels should obey the dictates of their own will. He sought to create sympathy for himself, by representing that God had dealt unjustly with him in bestowing supreme honor upon Christ. **He claimed that in aspiring to greater power and honor he was not aiming at self-exaltation, but was seeking to secure liberty for all the inhabitants of Heaven, that by this means they might attain to a higher state of existence.**

God, in His great mercy, bore long with Lucifer. He was not immediately degraded from his exalted station when he first indulged the spirit of discontent, nor even when he began to present his false claims before the loyal angels. Long was he retained in Heaven. Again and again he was offered pardon, on condition of repentance and submission. **Such efforts as only infinite love and wisdom could devise, were made to convince him of his error. The spirit of discontent had never before been known in Heaven. Lucifer himself did not at first see whither he was drifting**; he did not understand the real nature of his feelings. **But as his dissatisfaction was proved to be without cause, Lucifer was convinced that he was in the wrong, that the divine claims were just, and that he ought to acknowledge them as such before all Heaven. Had he done this, he might have saved himself and many angels.** He had not at this time fully cast off his allegiance to God. Though he had forsaken his position as covering cherub, yet if he had been willing to return to God, acknowledging the Creator's wisdom, and satisfied to fill the place appointed him in God's great plan, he would have been re-instated in his office. **But pride forbade him to submit. He persistently defended his own course, maintained that he had no need of repentance, and fully committed himself, in the great controversy, against his Maker.**

A Master of Deception

All the powers of his master-mind were now bent

to the work of deception, to secure the sympathy of the angels that had been under his command. Even the fact that Christ had warned and counseled him, was perverted to serve his traitorous designs. To those whose loving trust bound them most closely to him, Satan had represented that he was wrongly judged, that his position was not respected, and that his liberty was to be abridged. **From misrepresentation of the words of Christ, he passed to prevarication and direct falsehood**, accusing the Son of God of a design to humiliate him before the inhabitants of Heaven. He sought also to make a false issue between himself and the loyal angels. **All whom he could not subvert and bring fully to his side, he accused of indifference to the interests of heavenly beings. The very work which he himself was doing, he charged upon those who remained true to God.** And to sustain his charge of God's injustice toward him, he resorted to misrepresentation of the words and acts of the Creator. **It was his policy to perplex the angels with subtle arguments concerning the purposes of God. Everything that was simple he shrouded in mystery,** and by artful perversion cast doubt upon the plainest statements of Jehovah. His high position, in such close connection with the divine administration, gave greater force to his representations, and many were induced to unite with him in rebellion against Heaven's authority.

It Takes Time

God in His wisdom permitted Satan to carry forward his work, until the spirit of disaffection ripened into active revolt. It was necessary for his plans to be fully developed, that their true nature and tendency might be seen by all. Lucifer, as the anointed cherub, had been highly exalted; he was greatly loved by the heavenly beings, and his influence over them was strong. God's government included not only the inhabitants of Heaven, but of all the worlds that He had created; and **Satan thought that if he could carry the angels of Heaven with him in rebellion, he could carry also the**

other worlds. He had artfully presented his side of the question, employing sophistry and fraud to secure his objects. His power to deceive was very great, and by disguising himself in a cloak of falsehood he had gained an advantage. **Even the loyal angels could not fully discern his character, or see to what his work was leading.**

Satan had been so highly honored, and all his acts were so clothed with mystery, that it was difficult to disclose to the angels the true nature of his work. Until fully developed, sin would not appear the evil thing it was. Heretofore it had had no place in the universe of God, and holy beings had no conception of its nature and malignity. They could not discern the terrible consequences that would result from setting aside the divine law. **Satan had, at first, concealed his work under a specious profession of loyalty to God. He claimed to be seeking to promote the honor of God, the stability of His government, and the good of all the inhabitants of Heaven.** While instilling discontent into the minds of the angels under him, he had artfully made it appear that he was seeking to remove dissatisfaction. When he urged that changes be made in the order and laws of God's government, it was under the pretense that these were necessary in order to preserve harmony in Heaven.

In his dealing with sin, God could employ only righteousness and truth. Satan could use what God could not—flattery and deceit. He had sought to falsify the word of God, and had misrepresented His plan of government before the angels, claiming that God was not just in laying laws and rules upon the inhabitants of Heaven; that in requiring submission and obedience from His creatures, He was seeking merely the exaltation of himself. **Therefore it must be demonstrated before the inhabitants of Heaven as well as of all the worlds, that God's government was just, His law perfect.** Satan had made it appear that He Himself was seeking to promote the good of the universe. The true character of the usurper, and his real object, must be understood by all. He must have time to manifest himself by his wicked works.

The Work will Condemn

The discord which his own course had caused in Heaven, Satan charged upon the law and government of God. All evil he declared to be the result of the divine administration. He claimed that it was his own object to improve upon the statutes of Jehovah. Therefore it was necessary that he should demonstrate the nature of His claims, and show the working out of his proposed changes in the divine law. **His own work must condemn him. Satan had claimed from the first that he was not in rebellion. The whole universe must see the deceiver unmasked.**

Even when it was decided that he could no longer remain in Heaven, infinite wisdom did not destroy Satan. Since the service of love can alone be acceptable to God, the allegiance of His creatures must rest upon a conviction of His justice and benevolence. **The inhabitants of Heaven and of other worlds, being unprepared to comprehend the nature or consequences of sin, could not then have seen the justice and mercy of God in the destruction of Satan.** Had he been immediately blotted from existence, they would have served God from fear rather than from love. The influence of the deceiver would not have been fully destroyed, nor would the spirit of rebellion have been utterly eradicated. **Evil must be permitted to come to maturity. For the good of the entire universe through ceaseless ages, Satan must more fully develop his principles**, that his charges against the divine government might be seen in their true light by all created beings, that the justice and mercy of God and the immutability of His law might forever be placed beyond all question.

A Lesson for All Time

Satan's rebellion was to be a lesson to the universe through all coming ages, a perpetual testimony to the nature and terrible results of sin. The working out of

Satan's rule, its effects upon both men and angels, would show what must be the fruit of setting aside the divine authority. It would testify that with the existence of God's government and His law is bound up the well-being of all the creatures He has made. Thus the history of this terrible experiment of rebellion was to be a perpetual safeguard to all holy intelligences, to prevent them from being deceived as to the nature of transgression, to save them from committing sin, and suffering its punishment.

To the very close of the controversy in Heaven, the great usurper continued to justify himself. When it was announced that with all his sympathizers he must be expelled from the abodes of bliss, then the rebel leader boldly avowed his contempt for the Creator's law. He reiterated his claim that angels needed no control, but should be left to follow their own will, which would ever guide them right. **He denounced the divine statutes as a restriction of their liberty, and declared that it was his purpose to secure the abolition of law;** that, freed from this restraint, the hosts of Heaven might enter upon a more exalted, more glorious state of existence.

Cast Out of Heaven

With one accord, Satan and his host threw the blame of their rebellion wholly upon Christ, declaring that if they had not been reproved, they would never have rebelled. Thus stubborn and defiant in their disloyalty, seeking vainly to overthrow the government of God, yet blasphemously claiming to be themselves the innocent victims of oppressive power, **the arch-rebel and all his sympathizers were at last banished from Heaven.**

The same spirit that prompted rebellion in Heaven, still inspires rebellion on earth. Satan has continued with men the same policy which he pursued with the angels. His spirit now reigns in the children of disobedience. Like him they seek to break down the restraints of the law of God, and promise men liberty through transgression of its precepts. Reproof of sin still arouses the spirit of hatred and resistance. When God's messages of warning are brought home to the conscience, **Satan leads men to justify themselves and to seek the sympathy of others in their course of sin. Instead of correcting their errors, they excite indignation against the reprover**, as if he were the sole cause of difficulty. From the days of righteous Abel to our own time, such is the spirit which has been displayed toward those who dare to condemn sin.

Methods Unchanged

By the same misrepresentation of the character of God as he had practiced in Heaven, causing him to be regarded as severe and tyrannical, **Satan induced man to sin. And having succeeded thus far, he declared that God's unjust restrictions had led to man's fall, as they had led to his own rebellion.**

But the Eternal One Himself proclaims His character: "The Lord God, merciful and gracious, long-suffering, and abundant in goodness and truth, keeping mercy for thousands, forgiving iniquity and transgression and sin, and that will by no means clear the guilty." *Exodus 34:6-7.*

In the banishment of Satan from Heaven, God declared His justice, and maintained the honor of His throne. But when man had sinned through yielding to the deceptions of this apostate spirit, God gave an evidence of His love by yielding up His only begotten Son to die for the fallen race. In the atonement the character of God is revealed. The mighty argument of the cross demonstrates to the whole universe that the course of sin which Lucifer had chosen was in nowise chargeable upon the government of God.

Behold what Love and Hate

In the contest between Christ and Satan, during the Saviour's earthly ministry, the character of the great deceiver was unmasked. Nothing could so effectually have uprooted Satan from the affections of the heavenly angels and the whole loyal universe as

did his cruel warfare upon the world's Redeemer. The daring blasphemy of his demand that Christ should pay him homage, his presumptuous boldness in bearing Him to the mountain summit and the pinnacle of the temple, the malicious intent betrayed in urging Him to cast Himself down from the dizzy height, the unsleeping malice that hunted Him from place to place, inspiring the hearts of priests and people to reject His love, and at the last to cry, "Crucify Him! crucify Him!"—all this excited the amazement and indignation of the universe.

It was Satan that prompted the world's rejection of Christ. The prince of evil exerted all his power and cunning to destroy Jesus; for he saw that the Saviour's mercy and love, His compassion and pitying tenderness, were representing to the world the character of God. Satan contested every claim put forth by the Son of God, and employed men as His agents to fill the Saviour's life with suffering and sorrow. The sophistry and falsehood by which he had sought to hinder the work of Jesus, the hatred manifested through the children of disobedience, his cruel accusations against Him whose life was one of unexampled goodness, all sprung from deep-seated revenge. **The pent-up fires of envy and malice, hatred, and revenge burst forth on Calvary against the Son of God while all Heaven gazed upon the scene in silent horror.**

When the great sacrifice had been consummated, Christ ascended on high, refusing the adoration of angels until He had presented the request, "I will that they also, whom thou hast given Me, be with Me where I am" (John 17:24). Then with inexpressible love and power came forth the answer from the Father's throne, "Let all the angels of God worship Him" (Heb. 1:6). Not a stain rested upon Jesus. His humiliation ended, His sacrifice completed, there was given unto Him a name that is above every name.

Selfishness Unmasked

Now the guilt of Satan stood forth without excuse. He had revealed his true character as a liar and a

murderer. It was seen that the very same spirit with which he ruled the children of men, who were under his power, he would have manifested had he been permitted to control the inhabitants of Heaven. **He had claimed that the transgression of God's law would bring liberty and exaltation; but it was seen to result in bondage and degradation.**

Satan's lying charges against the divine character and government appeared in their true light. He had accused God of seeking merely the exaltation of Himself in requiring submission and obedience from His creatures, and had declared that while the Creator exacted self-denial from all others, He Himself practiced no self-denial, made no sacrifice. **Now it was seen that for the salvation of a fallen and sinful race, the Ruler of the universe had made the greatest sacrifice which love could make**; for "God was in Christ, reconciling the world unto Himself" (2 Cor. 5:19). It was seen, also, that while Lucifer had opened the door for the entrance of sin, by his desire for honor and supremacy, **Christ had, in order to destroy sin, humbled Himself and become obedient unto death.**

What God Is Like

God had manifested His abhorrence of the principles of rebellion. All Heaven saw His justice revealed, both in the condemnation of Satan and in the redemption of man. Lucifer had declared that if the law of God was changeless, and its penalty could not be remitted, every transgressor must be forever debarred from the Creator's favor. He had claimed that the sinful race were placed beyond redemption, and were therefore his rightful prey. **But the death of Christ was an argument in man's behalf that could not be overthrown.** The penalty of the law fell upon Him who was equal with God, and man was free to accept the righteousness of Christ, and by a life of penitence and humiliation to triumph, as the Son of God had triumphed, over the power of Satan. Thus God is just, and yet the justifier of all who believe in Jesus.

But it was not merely to accomplish the redemption of man that Christ came to the earth to suffer and to die. He came to "magnify the law" and to "make it honorable." Not alone that the inhabitants of this world might regard the law as it should be regarded; but it was to demonstrate to all the worlds of the universe that God's law is unchangeable. **Could its claims have been set aside, then the Son of God need not have yielded up His life to atone for its transgression. The death of Christ proves it immutable.** And the sacrifice to which infinite love impelled the Father and the Son, that sinners might be redeemed, demonstrates to all the universe—what nothing less than this plan of atonement could have sufficed to do—that justice and mercy are the foundation of the law and government of God.

It Will End in Ashes

In the final execution of the Judgment it will be seen that no cause for sin exists. When the Judge of all the earth shall demand of Satan, "Why hast thou rebelled against Me, and robbed Me of the subjects of My kingdom?" the originator of evil can render no excuse. Every mouth will be stopped, and all the hosts of rebellion will be speechless.

The cross of Calvary, while it declares the law immutable, proclaims to the universe that the wages of sin is death. In the Saviour's expiring cry, "It is finished," the death-knell of Satan was rung. The great controversy which had been so long in progress was then decided, and the final eradication of evil was made certain. The Son of God passed through the portals of the tomb, that "through death He might destroy him that had the power of death, that is, the devil" (Heb. 2:14). Lucifer's desire for self-exaltation had led him to say, "I will exalt my throne above the stars of God . . I will be like the Most High." God declares, "I will bring thee to ashes upon the earth . . and never shalt thou be any more" (Isa. 14:13-14; Eze. 28:18-19). When **"the day cometh that shall burn as an oven," "all the proud, yea, and all**

that do wickedly, shall be stubble; and the day that cometh shall burn them up, saith the Lord of hosts, that it shall leave them neither root nor branch" (Mal. 4:1).

Eternally Secure

The whole universe will have become witnesses to the nature and results of sin. And its utter extermination, which in the beginning would have brought fear to angels and dishonor to God, will now vindicate His love and establish His honor before a universe of beings who delight to do His will, and in whose heart is His law. Never will evil again be manifest. Says the Word of God, "Affliction shall not rise up the second time" (Nahum 1:9). The law of God, which Satan has reproached as the yoke of bondage, will be honored as the law of liberty. **A tested and proved creation will never again be turned from allegiance to Him whose character has been fully manifested before them as fathomless love and infinite wisdom.**

Enough May Be Understood

To many minds, the origin of sin and the reason for its existence are a source of great perplexity. They see the work of evil, with its terrible results of woe and desolation, and they question how all this can exist under the sovereignty of One who is infinite in wisdom, in power, and in love. Here is a mystery, of which they find no explanation. And in their uncertainty and doubt, they are blinded to truths plainly revealed in God's Word and essential to salvation. There are those who, in their inquiries concerning the existence of sin, endeavor to search into that which God has never revealed; hence they find no solution of their difficulties; and such as are actuated by a disposition to doubt and cavil, seize upon this as an excuse for rejecting the words of Holy Writ. Others, however, fail of a satisfactory understanding of the great problem of evil, from the fact that tradition and misinterpretation have obscured the teaching of the Bible concerning the character of God, the nature of His government, and the principles of His dealing with sin.

It is impossible to so explain the origin of sin as to give a reason for its existence. Yet enough may be understood concerning both the origin and the final disposition of sin, to fully make manifest the justice and benevolence of God in all His dealings with evil. Nothing is more plainly taught in Scripture than that **God was in nowise responsible for the entrance of sin**; that there was no arbitrary withdrawal of divine grace, no deficiency in the divine government, that gave occasion for the uprising of rebellion. **Sin is an intruder, for whose presence no reason can be given. It is mysterious, unaccountable; to excuse it is to defend it.** Could excuse for it be found, or cause be shown for its existence, it would cease to be sin. **Our only definition of sin is that given in the Word of God; it is "the transgression of the law";** it is the outworking of a principle at war with the great law of love which is the foundation of the divine government.

"This God is our God for ever and ever; He will be our guide even unto death."

—*Psalm 48:14*

"Unto Him that is able to keep you from falling, and to present you faultless before the presence of His glory with exceeding joy."

—*Jude 24*

"As the heaven is high above the earth, so great is His mercy toward them that fear Him."

—*Psalm 103:11*

"God is not ashamed to be called their God, for He hath prepared for them a city."

—*Hebrews 11:16*

— Chapter Two

Persecution in the First Centuries

— The Forming of the Beast

Seated on the Mount of Olives, Jesus foretold, to His disciples, years to come. He beheld the storms about to fall upon the young church; and, looking into the future, His eyes could see the fierce, wasting tempests that were to beat upon His followers in the ages of darkness that were ahead —

You are going to read the story of the whirlwind that came; the story of why it came; the story of men and women who lived through it—and died in it —

"If thou hadst known, even thou, at least in this thy day, the things which belong unto thy peace! but now they are hid from thine eyes. For the days shall come upon thee, that thine enemies shall cast a trench about thee, and compass thee round, and keep thee in on every side, and shall lay thee even with the ground, and thy children within thee; and they shall not leave in thee one stone upon another; because thou knewest not the time of thy visitation." *Luke 19:42-44.*

The disciples had been filled with awe and wonder at Christ's prediction of the overthrow of the temple, and they desired to understand more fully the meaning of His words. The Lord had told them that He would come the second time. Hence at the mention of judgments upon Jerusalem, their minds reverted to that coming, and as they were gathered about the Saviour upon the Mount of Olives, they asked, "When shall these things be? and what shall be the sign of Thy coming, and of the end of the world" (Matt. 24:3)?

Prophecy of the End

The future was mercifully veiled from the disciples. Had they at that time fully comprehended the two awful facts,—the Redeemer's sufferings and death and the destruction of their city and temple—they would have been overwhelmed with horror. Christ presented before them an outline of the prominent events to take place before the close of time. His words were not then fully understood; but their meaning was to be unfolded as His people should need the instruction therein given. The prophecy which He uttered was twofold in its meaning: while foreshadowing the destruction of Jerusalem, it prefigured also the terrors of the last great day. Jesus declared to the listening disciples the judgments that were to fall upon apostate Israel, and especially the retributive vengeance that would come upon them for their rejection and crucifixion of the Messiah. Unmistakable signs would precede the awful climax.

A Symbol of the World

Christ saw in Jerusalem a symbol of the world hardened in unbelief and rebellion, and hastening on to meet the retributive judgments of God. The woes of a fallen race, pressing upon His soul, forced from His lips that exceeding bitter cry. He saw the record of sin traced in human misery, tears, and blood; His heart was moved with infinite pity for the afflicted and suffering ones of earth; He yearned to relieve them all. But even His hand might not turn back the tide of human woe; few would seek their only source of help. He was willing to pour out His soul unto death, to bring salvation within their reach; but few would come to Him that they might have life.

The Majesty of Heaven in tears! The Son of the infinite God, troubled in spirit, bowed down with anguish! The scene filled all Heaven with wonder. That scene reveals to us the exceeding sinfulness of sin; it shows how hard a task it is, even for infinite power, to save the guilty from the consequences of transgressing the law of God. Jesus, looking down to the last generation, saw the world involved in a deception similar to that which caused the destruction of Jerusalem. The great sin of the Jews was their rejection of Christ; the great sin of the Christian world would be their rejection of the law of God, the foundation of His government in Heaven and earth. The precepts of Jehovah would be despised and set at naught. Millions in bondage to sin, slaves of Satan, doomed to suffer the second death, would refuse to listen to the words of truth in their day of visitation. Terrible blindness! Strange infatuation!

Another Fulfillment

The Saviour's prophecy concerning the visitation of judgments upon Jerusalem is to have another fulfillment, of which that terrible desolation was but a faint shadow. In the fate of the chosen city we may behold the doom of a world that has rejected God's mercy and trampled upon His law. Dark are the records of human misery that earth has witnessed during its long centuries of crime. The heart sickens and the mind grows faint in contemplation. Terrible have been the results of rejecting the authority of Heaven. But a scene yet darker is presented in the revelation of the future. The records of the past,—the long procession of tumults, conflicts, and revolutions, the "battle of the warrior is with confused noise, and garments rolled in blood" (Isa. 9:5). What are these, in contrast with the terrors of that day when the restraining Spirit of God shall be wholly withdrawn from the wicked, no longer to hold in check the outbursts of human passion and satanic wrath! The world will then behold, as never before, the results of Satan's rule.

As the Midnight Thief

The world is no more ready to credit the message for this time than were the Jews to receive the Saviour's warning concerning Jerusalem. Come when it may, the day of God will come unawares to the ungodly. When life is going on in its unvarying round; when men are absorbed in pleasure, in

business, in traffic, in money-making; when the religious
leaders are magnifying the world's progress and enlightenment, and the people are lulled in false security,—then, as
the midnight thief steals within the unguarded dwelling, so
shall sudden destruction come upon the careless and ungodly, "and they shall not escape" (1 Thess. 5:2-5).

Fierce Wasting Tempests

When Jesus revealed to His disciples the fate of
Jerusalem and the scenes of the second advent, He foretold also the experience of His people from the time when
He should be taken from them, to His return in power and
glory for their deliverance. From Olivet the Saviour beheld
the storms about to fall upon the apostolic church; and,
penetrating deeper into the future, His eye discerned the
fierce, wasting tempests that were to beat upon His followers in the coming ages of darkness and persecution. In
a few brief utterances of awful significance, He foretold
the portion which the rulers of this world would mete out to
the church of God (Matt. 24:9, 21-22). The followers of
Christ must tread the same path of humiliation, reproach,
and suffering which their Master trod. The enmity that burst
forth against the world's Redeemer would be manifested
against all who should believe on His name.

The history of the early church testified to the fulfillment of the Saviour's words. The powers of earth and hell
arrayed themselves against Christ in the person of His followers. Paganism foresaw that should the gospel triumph,
her temples and altars would be swept away; therefore
she summoned her forces to destroy Christianity. The fires
of persecution were kindled. Christians were stripped of
their possessions, and driven from their homes. They "endured a great fight of afflictions" (Heb. 10:32). They "had
trial of cruel mockings and scourgings, yea, moreover of
bonds and imprisonment" (Heb. 11:36). Great numbers
sealed their testimony with their blood. Noble and slave,
rich and poor, learned and ignorant, were alike slain without mercy.

Blood Is Seed

Under the fiercest persecution, these witnesses for Jesus kept their faith unsullied. A voice came down to them from the throne of God, "Be thou faithful unto death, and I will give thee a crown of life" (Rev. 2:10). In vain were Satan's efforts to destroy the church of Christ by violence. The great controversy in which the disciples of Jesus yielded up their lives did not cease when these faithful standard bearers fell at their post. By defeat they conquered. God's workmen were slain, but His work went steadily forward. The gospel continued to spread, and the number of its adherents to increase. It penetrated into regions that were inaccessible, even to the eagles of Rome. Said a Christian, expostulating with the heathen rulers who were urging forward the persecution: "You may torment, afflict, and vex us. Your wickedness puts our weakness to the test, but your cruelty is of no avail. It is but a stronger invitation to bring others to our persuasion. The more we are mowed down, the more we spring up again. The blood of the Christians is seed."

Thousands were imprisoned and slain; but others sprung up to fill their places. And those who were martyred for their faith were secured to Christ and accounted of Him as conquerors. They had fought the good fight, and they were to receive the crown of glory when Christ should come. The sufferings which they endured brought Christians nearer to one another and to their Redeemer. Their living example and dying testimony were a constant witness for the truth; and, where least expected, the subjects of Satan were leaving his service and enlisting under the banner of Christ.

Deception instead of Persecution

Satan therefore laid his plans to war more successfully against the government of God, by planting his banner in the Christian church. If the followers of Christ could be deceived, and led to displease God, then their strength, fortitude, and firmness would fail, and they would fall an easy prey.

The great adversary now endeavored to gain by artifice what he had failed to secure by force. Persecution ceased, and in its stead were substituted the dangerous allurements of temporal prosperity and worldly honor. Idolaters were led to receive a part of the Christian faith while they rejected other essential truths. They professed to accept Jesus as the Son of God, and to believe in His death and resurrection; but they had no conviction of sin, and felt no need of repentance or of a change of heart. With some concessions on their part, they proposed that Christians should make concessions, that all might unite on the platform of belief in Christ.

Fearful Peril

Now the church was in fearful peril. Prison, torture, fire, and sword were blessings in comparison with this. Some of the Christians stood firm, declaring that they could make no compromise. Others were in favor of yielding or modifying some features of their faith and uniting with those who had accepted a part of Christianity, urging that this might be the means of their full conversion. That was a time of deep anguish to the faithful followers of Christ. Under a cloak of pretended Christianity, Satan was insinuating himself into the church, to corrupt their faith and turn their minds from the Word of truth.

Most of the Christians at last consented to lower their standard, and a union was formed between Christianity and paganism. Although the worshipers of idols professed to be converted and united with the church, they still clung to their idolatry, only changing the objects of their worship to images of Jesus, and even of Mary and the saints. The foul leaven of idolatry, thus brought into the church, continued its baleful work. Unsound doctrines, superstitious rites, and idolatrous ceremonies were incorporated into her faith and worship. As the followers of Christ united with idolaters, the Christian religion became corrupted, and the church lost her purity and power. There were some, however, who were not misled by these delusions. They still maintained their fidelity to the Author of truth, and worshiped God alone.

Desperate Struggle

It required a desperate struggle for those who would be faithful to stand firm against the deceptions and abominations which were disguised in sacerdotal garments and introduced into the church. The Bible was not accepted as the standard of faith. The doctrine of religious freedom was termed heresy, and its upholders were hated and proscribed.

After a long and severe conflict, the faithful few decided to dissolve all union with the apostate church if she still refused to free herself from falsehood and idolatry. They saw that separation was an absolute necessity if they would obey the Word of God. They dared not tolerate errors fatal to their own souls, and set an example which would imperil the faith of their children and children's children. To secure peace and unity they were ready to make any concession consistent with fidelity to God; but they felt that even peace would be too dearly purchased at the sacrifice of principle. If unity could be secured only by the compromise of truth and righteousness, then let there be difference, and even war.

The Great Apostasy

The apostle Paul, in his second letter to the Thessalonians, foretold the great apostasy which would result in the establishment of the papal power. He declared that the day of Christ should not come, "except there come a falling away first, and that man of sin be revealed, the son of perdition; who opposeth and exalteth himself above all that is called God, or that is worshipped; so that he as God sitteth in the temple of God, showing himself that he is God" (2 Thess. 2:3-4). And furthermore, the apostle warns his brethren that "the mystery of iniquity doth already work" (2 Thess. 2:7). Even at that early date he saw, creeping into the church, errors that would prepare the way for the development of the papacy.

Little by little, at first in stealth and silence, and then

more openly as it increased in strength and gained control of the minds of men, the mystery of iniquity carried forward its deceptive and blasphemous work. Almost imperceptibly the customs of heathenism found their way into the Christian church. The spirit of compromise and conformity was restrained for a time by the fierce persecutions which the church endured under paganism. But as persecution ceased, and Christianity entered the courts and palaces of kings, she laid aside the humble simplicity of Christ and His apostles for the pomp and pride of pagan priests and rulers; and in place of the requirements of God, she substituted human theories and traditions. The nominal conversion of Constantine, in the early part of the fourth century, caused great rejoicing; and the world, cloaked with a form of righteousness, walked into the church. Now the work of corruption rapidly progressed. Paganism, while appearing to be vanquished, became the conqueror. Her spirit controlled the church. Her doctrines, ceremonies, and superstitions were incorporated into the faith and worship of the professed followers of Christ.

The Man of Sin

This compromise between paganism and Christianity resulted in the development of the "man of sin" foretold in prophecy as opposing and exalting himself above God. That gigantic system of false religion is a masterpiece of Satan's power,—a monument of his efforts to seat himself upon the throne to rule the earth according to his will.

Change Times and Laws

The detector of error having been removed, Satan worked according to his will. Prophecy had declared that the papacy was to "think to change times and laws" (Dan. 7:25). This work was not slow to attempt. To afford converts from heathenism a substitute for the worship of idols, and thus to promote their nominal acceptance of Christianity, the adoration of images and relics was gradually introduced into the Christian worship. The decree of a general council (Second Council of Nice, A.D. 787) finally estabished this system of idolatry. To complete the sacrilegious work, Rome presumed to expunge from the law of God the second commandment, forbidding image worship, and to divide the tenth commandment, in order to preserve the number.

The spirit of concession to paganism opened the way for a still further disregard of Heaven's authority. Satan tampered with the fourth Commandment also, and essayed to set aside the ancient Sabbath, the day which God had blessed and sanctified (Gen. 2:2-3), and in its stead to exalt the festival observed by the heathen as "the venerable day of the sun." This change was not at first attempted openly. In the first centuries the true Sabbath had been kept by all Christians. They were jealous for the honor of God and, believing that His law is immutable, they zealously guarded the sacredness of its precepts. But with great subtlety, Satan worked through his agents to bring about his object. That the attention of the people might be called to the Sunday, it was made a festival in honor of the resurrection of Christ. Religious services were held upon it; yet it was regarded as a day of recreation, the Sabbath being still sacredly observed.

To prepare the way for the work which he designed to accomplish, Satan had led the Jews, before the advent of Christ, to load down the Sabbath with the most rigorous exactions, making its observance a burden. Now, taking advantage of the false light in which he had thus caused it to be regarded, he cast contempt upon it as a Jewish institution. While Christians continued to observe the Sunday as a joyous festival, he led them, in order to show their hatred of Judaism, to make the Sabbath a fast, a day of sadness and gloom.

The Day of the Sun

In the early part of the fourth century, the emperor Constantine issued a decree making Sunday a public festival throughout the Roman Empire. The day of the sun was reverenced by his pagan subjects, and was honored by Christians; it was the emperor's policy to unite the conflicting interests of heathenism and Christianity. He was urged to do this by the bishops of the church, who, inspired by ambition and thirst for power, perceived that if the same day was observed by both Christians and the heathen, it would promote the nominal acceptance of Christianity by pagans and thus advance the power and glory of the church. But while Christians were gradually led to regard Sunday as possessing a degree of sacredness, they still held the true Sabbath as the holy of the Lord, and observed it in obedience to the fourth commandment.

The Commandments of Men

The arch-deceiver had not completed his work. He was resolved to gather the Christian world under his banner and to exercise his power through his vicegerent, the proud pontiff who claimed to be the representative of Christ. Through half-converted pagans, ambitious prelates, and world-loving churchmen, he accomplished his purpose. Vast councils were held from time to time, in which the dignitaries of the church were convened from all the world. In nearly every council the Sabbath which God had instituted was pressed down a little lower while the Sunday was correspondingly exalted. Thus the pagan festival came finally to be honored as a divine institution while the Bible Sabbath was pronounced a relic of Judaism and its observers were declared to be accursed.

The great apostate had succeeded in exalting himself "above all that is called God, or that is worshiped" (2 Thess. 2:4). He had dared to change the only precept of the divine law that unmistakably points all mankind to the true and living God. In the fourth commandment, God is revealed as the Creator of the heavens and the earth, and is thereby distinguished from all false gods. It was as a memorial of the work of creation that the seventh day was sanctified as a rest day for man. It was designed to keep the living God ever before the minds of men as the source of being and the object of reverence and worship. Satan strives to turn men from their allegiance to God and from rendering obedience to His law; therefore he directs his efforts especially against that commandment which points to God as the Creator.

Child of the Papacy

Protestants now urge that the resurrection of Christ on Sunday made it the Christian Sabbath. But Scripture evidence is lacking. No such honor was given to the day by Christ or His apostles. The observance of Sunday as a Christian institution had its origin in that "mystery of lawlessness" (2 Thess. 2:7, R.V.), which even in Paul's day, had begun its work. Where and when did the Lord adopt this child of the papacy? What valid reason can be given for a change which the Scriptures do not sanction?

Papal Supremacy

In the sixth century the papacy had become firmly established. Its seat of power was fixed in the imperial city, and the bishop of Rome was declared to be the head over the entire church. Paganism had given place to the papacy. The dragon had given to the beast "his power, and his seat, and great authority" (Rev. 13:2). And now began the 1260 years of papal oppression foretold in the prophecies of Daniel and the Revelation (Dan. 7:25; Rev. 13:5-7). Christians were forced to choose, either to yield their integrity and accept the papal ceremonies and worship or to wear away their lives in dungeons or suffer death by the rack, the fagot, or the headsman's ax. Now were fulfilled the words of Jesus, "Ye shall be betrayed both by parents, and brethren, and kinsfolks, and friends; and some of you shall they cause to be put to death. And ye shall be hated of all men for My name's sake" (Luke 21:16-17). Persecution opened upon the faithful with greater fury than ever before, and the world became a vast battlefield. For hundreds of years the church of Christ found refuge in seclusion and obscurity. Thus says the prophet: "The woman fled into the wilderness, where she hath a place prepared of God, that they should feed her there a thousand two hundred and threescore days." *Revelation 12:6.*

The Dark Ages

The accession of the Roman Church to power marked the beginning of the Dark Ages. As her power increased, the darkness deepened. Faith was transferred from Christ, the true foundation, to the pope of Rome. Instead of trusting in the Son of God for forgiveness of sins and for eternal salvation, the people looked to the pope and to the priests and prelates to whom he delegated authority. They were taught that the pope was their earthly mediator, and that none could approach God except through him; and, further, that he stood in the place of God to them, and was therefore to be implicitly obeyed. A deviation from his requirements was sufficient cause for the severest punishment to be visited upon the bodies and souls of the offenders. Thus the minds of the people were turned away from God to fallible, erring, and cruel men; nay more, to the prince of darkness himself, who exercised his power through them. Sin was disguised in a garb of sanctity. When the Scriptures are suppressed, and man comes to regard himself as supreme, we need look only for fraud, deception, and debasing iniquity. With the elevation of human laws and traditions was manifest the corruption that ever results from setting aside the law of God.

Flight into the Wilderness

Among the leading causes that had led to the separation of the true church from Rome was the hatred of the latter toward the Bible Sabbath. As foretold by prophecy, the papal power cast down the truth to the ground. The law of God was trampled in the dust while the traditions and customs of men were exalted. The churches that were under the rule of the papacy were early compelled to honor the Sunday as a holy day. Amid the prevailing error and superstition, many, even of the true people of God, became so bewildered that while they observed the Sabbath they refrained from labor also on the Sunday. But this did not satisfy the papal leaders. They demanded not only that Sunday be hallowed, but that the Sabbath be profaned; and they denounced in the strongest language those who dared to show it honor. It was only by fleeing from the power of Rome that any could obey God's law in peace.

In Lands Beyond

In lands beyond the jurisdiction of Rome, there existed for many centuries bodies of Christians who remained almost wholly free from papal corruption. They were surrounded by heathenism, and in the lapse of ages were affected by its errors; but they continued to regard the Bible as the only rule of faith, and adhered to many of its truths. These Christians believed in the perpetuity of the law of God and observed the Sabbath of the fourth commandment. Churches that held to this faith and practice existed in Central Africa and among the Armenians of Asia.

The Waldenses

But of those who resisted the encroachments of the papal power, the Waldenses stood foremost. In the very land where popery had fixed its seat, there its falsehood and corruption were most steadfastly resisted . . The persecutions visited for many centuries upon this God-fearing people were endured by them with a patience and constancy that honored their Redeemer. Notwithstanding the crusades against them, and the inhuman butchery to which they were subjected, they continued to send out their missionaries to scatter the precious truth. They were hunted to the death; yet their blood watered the seed sown, and it failed not of yielding fruit. Thus the Waldenses witnessed for God, centuries before the birth of Luther. Scattered over many lands, they planted the seeds of the Reformation that began in the time of Wycliffe, grew broad and deep in the days of Luther, and is to be carried forward to the close of time by those who also are willing to suffer all things for "the Word of God and for the testimony of Jesus Christ" (Rev. 1:9).

The Reformation Continues

The Reformation did not, as many suppose, end with Luther. It is to be continued to the close of this world's history. Luther had a great work to do in reflecting to others the light which God had permitted to shine upon him; yet he did not receive all the light which was to be given to the world. From that time to this, new light has been continually shining upon the Scriptures, and new truths have been constantly unfolding.

Bridging the Chasm

The English Reformers, while renouncing the doctrines of Romanism, had retained many of its forms. Thus though the authority and the creed of Rome were rejected, not a few of her customs and ceremonies were incorporated into the worship of the Church of England. It was claimed that these things were not matters of conscience, that though they were not commanded in Scripture, and hence were nonessential, yet not being forbidden, they were not intrinsically evil. Their observance tended to narrow the gulf which separated the Reformed churches from Rome, and it was urged that they would promote the acceptance of the Protestant faith by Romanists. To the conservative and compromising, these arguments seemed conclusive. But there was another class that did not so judge. The fact that these customs tended to bridge the chasm between Rome and the Reformation was in their view a conclusive argument against retaining them. They looked upon them as badges of the slavery from which they had been delivered, and to which they had no disposition to return. They reasoned that God has in His Word established the regulations governing His worship, and that men are not at liberty to add to these or to detract from them. The very beginning of the great apostasy was in seeking to supplement the authority of God by that of the church. Rome began by enjoining what God had not forbidden, and she ended by forbidding what He had explicitly enjoined.

Sealing the Law

The work of Sabbath reform to be accomplished in the last days is foretold in the prophecy of Isaiah: "Thus saith the Lord, Keep ye judgment, and do justice: for My salvation is near to come, and My righteousness to be revealed. Blessed is the man that doeth this, and the son of man that layeth hold on it; that keepeth the Sabbath from polluting it, and keepeth his hand from doing any evil." "The sons of the stranger, that join themselves to the Lord . . to be His servants, every one that keepeth the Sabbath from polluting it, and taketh hold of My covenant; even them will I bring to My holy mountain, and make them joyful in My house of prayer." *Isaiah 56:1-2, 6-7.*

These words apply in the Christian age, as is shown by the context: "The Lord God which gathereth the outcasts of Israel saith, Yet will I gather others to him, beside those that are gathered unto him." *Isaiah 56:8.* Here is foreshadowed the gathering in of the Gentiles by the gospel. And upon those who then honor the Sabbath, a blessing is pronounced. Thus the obligation of the fourth commandment extends past the crucifixion, resurrection, and ascension of Christ, to the time when His servants should preach to all nations the message of glad tidings.

The Lord commands by the same prophet, "Bind up the testimony, seal the law among My disciples" (Isa. 8:16). The seal of God's law is found in the fourth commandment. This only, of all the ten, brings to view both the name and the title of the Lawgiver. It declares Him to be the Creator of the heavens and the earth, and thus shows His claim to reverence and worship above all others. Aside from this precept, there is nothing in the decalogue to show by whose authority the law is given. When the Sabbath was changed by the papal power, the seal was taken from the law. The disciples of Jesus are called upon to restore it, by exalting the Sabbath of the fourth commandment to its rightful position as the Creator's memorial and the sign of His authority.

"To the law and to the testimony." While conflicting doctrines and theories abound, the law of God is the one unerring rule by which all opinions, doctrines, and theories are to be tested. Says the prophet, "If they speak not according to this Word, it is because there is no light in them" (Isa. 8:20).

The prophet thus points out the ordinance which has

been forsaken: "Thou shalt raise up the foundations of many generations; and thou shalt be called the repairer of the breach, the restorer of paths to dwell in. If thou turn away thy foot from the Sabbath, from doing thy pleasure on My holy day; and call the Sabbath a delight, the holy of the Lord, honorable; and shalt honor Him, not doing thine own ways, nor finding thine own pleasure, nor speaking thine own words; then shalt thou delight thyself in the Lord." *Isaiah 58:12-14.* This prophecy also applies in our time. The breach was made in the law of God when the Sabbath was changed by the Roman power. But the time has come for that divine institution to be restored. The breach is to be repaired, and the foundation of many generations to be raised up.

Hallowed by the Creator's rest and blessing, the Sabbath was kept by Adam in his innocence in holy Eden; by Adam, fallen yet repentant, when he was driven from his happy estate. It was kept by all the patriarchs, from Abel to righteous Noah, to Abraham, to Jacob. When the chosen people were in bondage in Egypt, many, in the midst of prevailing idolatry, lost their knowledge of God's law; but when the Lord delivered Israel, He proclaimed His law in awful grandeur to the assembled multitude, that they might know His will, and fear and obey Him forever.

From that day to the present, the knowledge of God's law has been preserved in the earth, and the Sabbath of the fourth commandment has been kept. Though the "man of sin" succeeded in trampling underfoot God's holy day, yet even in the period of his supremacy there were, hidden in secret places, faithful souls who paid it honor. Since the Reformation, there have been some in every generation to maintain its observance. Though often in the midst of reproach and persecution, a constant testimony has been borne to the perpetuity of the law of God and the sacred obligation of the creation Sabbath.

Truth Is Older than Error

Many urged that Sundaykeeping had been an estab

lished doctrine and a widespread custom of the church for many centuries. Against this argument it was shown that the Sabbath and its observance were more ancient and widespread, even as old as the world itself, and bearing the sanction both of angels and of God. When the foundations of the earth were laid, when the morning stars sang together, and all the sons of God shouted for joy, then was laid the foundation of the Sabbath (Job 38:6-7; Gen. 2:1-3). Well may this institution demand our reverence: it was ordained by no human authority, and rests upon no human traditions; it was established by the Ancient of days, and commanded by His eternal Word.

"Blessed are they that do His commandments, that they may have right to the tree of life, and may enter in through the gates into the city."

—*Revelation 22:14*

"My God shall supply all your need according to His riches in glory by Christ Jesus." —*Philippians 4:19*

"Great peace have they which love Thy law, and nothing shall offend them."

—*Psalm 119:165*

"Take My yoke upon you, and learn of Me, for I am meek and lowly in heart; and ye shall find rest unto your souls."

—*Matthew 11:29*

Chapter Three

Preparing for the Mark

—Laying Plans to Destroy

One of the most solemn warnings ever given in Scripture is to be found in the thirteenth and fourteenth chapters of the book of Revelation. What IS the Mark of the Beast? When will it be given? Who will receive it? And most important, what must you and I do in order to avoid receiving it?

This is a subject of overwhelming importance. It contains facts you should know. We are living very near the end of time, and thinking men recognize that an immense crisis is rapidly approaching —

Those who had accepted the light concerning the mediation of Christ and the perpetuity of the law of God found that these were the truths presented in Revelation 14. The messages of this chapter constitute a threefold warning, which is to prepare the inhabitants of the earth for the Lord's second coming.

The Hour of His Judgment

The announcement, "The hour of His Judgment is come," points to the closing work of Christ's ministration for the salvation of men. It heralds a truth which must be proclaimed until the Saviour's intercession shall cease, and He shall return to the earth to take His people to Himself. The work of judgment, which began in 1844, must continue until the cases of all are decided, both of the living and the dead; hence it will extend to the close of human probation. That men may be prepared to stand in the Judgment, the message commands them to "fear God, and give glory to

Him," "and worship Him that made heaven, and earth, and the sea, and the fountains of waters." The result of an acceptance of these messages is given in the words, "Here are they that keep the commandments of God and the faith of Jesus."

In order to be prepared for the Judgment, it is necessary that men should keep the law of God. That law will be the standard of character in the Judgment. The apostle Paul declares, "As many as have sinned in the law shall be judged by the law . . in the day when God shall judge the secrets of men by Jesus Christ" (Rom. 2:12, 16). And he says that "the doers of the law shall be justified." Faith is essential in order to keep of the law of God; for "without faith it is impossible to please Him." And "whatsoever is not of faith is sin" (Heb. 11:6; Rom. 14:23).

By the first angel, men are called upon to "fear God, and give glory to Him," and to worship Him as the Creator of the heavens and the earth. In order to do this, they must obey His law. Says the wise man, "Fear God, and keep His commandments; for this is the whole duty of man" (Eccl. 12:13). Without obedience to His commandments, no worship can be pleasing to God. "This is the love of God, that we keep His commandments." "He that turneth away his ear from hearing the law, even his prayer shall be abomination." *1 John 5:3; Proverbs 28:9.*

Worship the Creator

The duty to worship God is based upon the fact that He is the Creator, and that to Him all other beings owe their existence. And wherever, in the Bible, His claim to reverence and worship above the gods of the heathen is presented, there is cited the evidence of His creative power. "All the gods of the nations are idols; but the Lord made the heavens." *Psalm 96:5.* "To whom then will ye liken Me, or shall I be equal? saith the Holy One. Lift up your eyes on high, and behold who hath created these things." "Thus saith the Lord that created the heavens; God Himself that formed the earth and made it . . I am the Lord; and there is none else." *Isaiah 40:25-26; 45:18.* Says

the psalmist: "Know ye that the Lord, He is God: it is He
that hath made us, and not we ourselves." "O come, let us
worship and bow down: let us kneel before the Lord our
Maker." *Psalms 100:3; 95:6*. And the holy beings who
worship God in Heaven state, as the reason why their homage is due to Him, "Thou art worthy, O Lord, to receive
glory and honor and power: for Thou hast created all things"
(Rev. 4:11).

In Revelation 14, men are called upon to worship the
Creator; and the prophecy brings to view a class that, as
the result of the threefold message, are keeping the commandments of God. One of these commandments points
directly to God as the Creator. The fourth precept declares:
"The seventh day is the Sabbath of the Lord thy God . . For
in six days the Lord made heaven and earth, the sea, and
all that in them is, and rested the seventh day; wherefore
the Lord blessed the Sabbath day, and hallowed it." *Exodus 20:10-11*. Concerning the Sabbath, the Lord says further: that it is "a sign . . that ye may know that I am the
Lord your God" (Eze. 20:20). And the reason given is: "For
in six days the Lord made heaven and earth, and on the
seventh day He rested and was refreshed" (Ex. 31:17).

Sabbath - Worship - Creator

"The importance of the Sabbath as the memorial of
creation is that it keeps ever present the true reason why
worship is due to God,"—because He is the Creator and
we His creatures. "The Sabbath therefore lies at the very
foundation of divine worship; for it teaches this great truth
in the most impressive manner, and no other institution does
this. The true ground of divine worship, not of that on the
seventh day merely, but of all worship, is found in the distinction between the Creator and His creatures. This great
fact can never become obsolete, and must never be forgotten." It was to keep this truth ever before the minds of
men that God instituted the Sabbath in Eden; and so long as
the fact that He is our Creator continues to be a reason
why we should worship Him, so long the Sabbath will continue as its sign and memorial. Had the Sabbath been uni-

versally kept, man's thoughts and affections would have been led to the Creator as the object of reverence and worship, and there would never have been an idolater, an atheist, or an infidel. The keeping of the Sabbath is a sign of loyalty to the true God, "Him that made heaven and earth, and the sea, and the fountains of waters." It follows that the message which commands men to worship God and keep His commandments will especially call upon them to keep the fourth commandment.

If Any Man Worship the Beast

In contrast to those who keep the commandments of God and have the faith of Jesus, the third angel points to another class, against whose errors a solemn and fearful warning is uttered: "If any man worship the beast and his image, and receive his mark in his forehead, or in his hand, the same shall drink of the wine of the wrath of God." *Revelation 14:9-10.* A correct interpretation of the symbols employed is necessary to an understanding of this message. What is represented by the beast, the image, the mark?

The line of prophecy in which these symbols are found begins with Revelation 12, with the dragon that sought to destroy Christ at His birth. The dragon is said to be Satan (Rev. 12:9); he it was that moved upon Herod to put the Saviour to death. But the chief agent of Satan in making war upon Christ and His people during the first centuries of the Christian era was the Roman Empire, in which paganism was the prevailing religion. Thus, while the dragon primarily represents Satan, it is, in a secondary sense, a symbol of pagan Rome.

The Beast of Revelation 13

In Chapter 13 (verses 1-10) is described another beast, "like unto a leopard," to which the dragon gave "his power, and his seat, and great authority." This symbol, as most Protestants have believed, represents the papacy, which succeeded to the power and seat and authority once possessed by the ancient Roman Empire. Of the leopard-like beast it is declared: "There was given unto him a mouth speaking great things and blasphemies . . And he opened his mouth in blasphemy against God, to blaspheme His name, and His tabernacle, and them that dwell in Heaven. And it was given unto him to make war with the saints, and to overcome them; and power was given him over all kindreds, and tongues, and nations." *Revelation 13:5-7*. This prophecy, which is nearly identical with the description of the little horn of Daniel 7, unquestionably points to the papacy.

Forty and Two Months

"Power was given unto him to continue forty and two months." And, says the prophet, "I saw one of his heads as it were wounded to death." And again. "He that leadeth into captivity shall go into captivity; he that killeth with the sword must be killed with the sword." The forty and two months are the same as the "time and times and the dividing of time," three years and a half, or 1260 days, of Daniel 7,—the time during which the papal power was to oppress God's people. This period, as stated in preceding chapters, began with the establishment of the papacy, A.D. 538, and terminated in 1798. At that time, when the papacy was abolished and the pope made captive by the French army, the papal power received its deadly wound, and the prediction was fulfilled, "He that leadeth into captivity shall go into captivity."

Lamb-like Beast

At this point another symbol is introduced. Says the prophet, "I beheld another beast coming up out of the earth; and he had two horns like a lamb" (Rev. 13:11). Both the appearance of this beast and the manner of its rise indicate that the nation which it represents is unlike those presented under the preceding symbols. The great kingdoms that have ruled the world were presented to the prophet Daniel as beasts of prey, rising when the "four winds of the heaven strove upon the great sea" (Dan. 7:2). In Revelation 17, an angel explained that waters represent "peoples, and multitudes, and nations, and tongues" (Rev. 17:15). Winds are a symbol of strife. The four winds of heaven, striving upon the great sea, represent the terrible scenes of conquest and revolution by which kingdoms have attained to power.

Out of the Earth

But the beast with the lamb-like horns was seen "coming up out of the earth." Instead of overthrowing other powers to establish itself, the nation thus represented must arise in territory previously unoccupied, and grow up gradually and peacefully. It could not, then, arise among the crowded and struggling nationalities of the Old World,—that turbulent sea of "peoples, and multitudes, and nations, and tongues." It must be sought in the Western Continent.

What nation of the New World was in 1798 rising into power, giving promise of strength and greatness, and attracting the attention of the world? The application of the symbol admits of no question. One nation, and only one, meets the specifications of this prophecy; it points unmistakably to the United States of America. Again and again the thought, almost the exact words, of the sacred writer have been unconsciously employed by the orator and the historian in describing the rise and growth of this nation. The beast was seen "coming up out of the earth"; and, according to the translators, the word here rendered "coming up" literally signifies to "grow or spring up as a plant." And, as we have seen, the nation must arise in territory previously unoccupied. A prominent writer—describing the rise of the United States—speaks of "the mystery of her coming forth from vacancy," and says, "Like a silent seed we grew into empire" (*Townsend, in The New World Compared with the Old, p. 462*). A European journal in 1850 spoke of the United States as a wonderful empire, which was "emerging," and "amid the silence of the earth daily adding to its power and pride" (*The Dublin Nation*). Edward Everett, in an oration on the Pilgrim founders of this nation, said: "Did they look for a retired spot, inoffensive from its obscurity, safe in its remoteness from the haunts of despots, where the little church of Leyden might enjoy freedom of conscience? Behold the mighty regions over which, in peaceful conquest . . they have borne the banners of the cross."

Like a Lamb

"And he had two horns like a lamb." The lamb-like horns indicate youth, innocence, and gentleness, fitly representing the character of the United States when presented to the prophet as "coming up" in 1798. The Christian exiles who first fled to America sought an asylum from royal oppression and priestly intolerance, and they determined to establish a government upon the broad foundation of civil and religious liberty. The Declaration of Independence sets forth the great truth that "all men are created equal" and endowed with the inalienable right to "life, liberty, and the pursuit of happiness." And the Constitution guarantees to the people the right of self-government, providing that representatives elected by the popular vote shall enact and administer the laws. Freedom of religious faith was also granted, every man being permitted to worship God according to the dictates of his conscience. Republicanism and Protestantism became the fundamental principles of the nation. These principles are the secret of its power and prosperity. The oppressed and down-trodden throughout Christendom have turned to this land with interest and hope. Millions have sought its shores, and the United States has risen to a place among the most powerful nations of the earth.

Spake as a Dragon

But the beast with lamb-like horns and dragon voice of the symbol point to a striking contradiction between the professions and the practice of the nation thus represented. The "speaking" of the nation is the action of its legislative and judicial authorities. By such action it will give the lie to those liberal and peaceful principles which it has put forth as the foundation of its policy. The prediction that it will speak "as a dragon," and exercise "all the power of the first beast," plainly foretells a development of the spirit of intolerance and persecution that was manifested by the nations represented by the dragon and the leopard-like beast. And the statement that the beast with two horns "causeth the earth and them which dwell therein to worship the first beast," indicates that the authority of this nation is to be exercised in enforcing some observance which shall be an act of homage to the papacy.

Such action would be directly contrary to the principles of this government, to the genius of its free institutions, to the direct and solemn avowals of the Declaration of Independence, and to the Constitution. The founders of the nation wisely sought to guard against the employment of the secular power on the part of the church, with its inevitable result—intolerance and persecution. The Constitution provides that "Congress shall make no law respecting an establishment of religion, or prohibiting the free exercise thereof," and that "no religious test shall ever be required as a qualification to any office of public trust under the United States." Only in flagrant violation of these safeguards to the nation's liberty can any religious observance be enforced by civil authority. But the inconsistency of such action is no greater than is represented in the symbol. It is the beast with lamb-like horns—in profession pure, gentle, and harmless—that speaks as a dragon.

Make an Image

"Saying to them that dwell on the earth, that *they* should make an image to the beast." Here is clearly presented a form of government in which the legislative power rests with the people, a most striking evidence that the United States is the nation denoted in the prophecy.

But what is the "image to the beast"? and how is it to be formed? The image is made by the two-horned beast, and is an image *to* the first beast. Then to learn what the image is like, and how it is to be formed, we must study the characteristics of the beast itself,—the papacy. When the early church became corrupted by departing from the simplicity of the gospel, and accepting heathen rites and customs, she lost the Spirit and power of God; and in order to control the consciences of the people, she sought the support of the secular power. The result was the papacy, a church that controlled the power of the State, and employed it to further her own ends, especially for the punishment of "heresy." In order for the United States to form an image to the beast, the religious power must so control the civil government that the authority of the State will also be employed by the church to accomplish her own ends.

Whenever the church has obtained secular power, she has employed it to punish dissent from her doctrines. Apostasy in the church will prepare the way for the image to the beast.

When the leading churches of the United States, uniting upon such points of doctrine as are held by them in common, shall influence the State to enforce their decrees and to sustain their institutions, then Protestant America will have formed an image of the Roman hierarchy, and the infliction of civil penalties upon dissenters will inevitably result.

The Third Angel's Warning

The beast with two horns "causeth [commands] all, both small and great, rich and poor, free and bond, to receive a mark in their right hand, or in their foreheads: and that no man might buy or sell, save he that had the mark, or the name of the beast, or the number of his name" (Rev. 13:16-17). The third angel's warning is: "If any man worship the beast and his image, and receive his mark in his forehead, or in his hand, the same shall drink of the wine of the wrath of God." "The beast" mentioned in this message, whose worship is enforced by the two-horned beast, is the first, or leopard-like beast of Revelation 13,—the papacy. The "image to the beast" represents that form of apostate Protestantism which will be developed when the Protestant churches shall seek the aid of the civil power for the enforcement of their dogmas. The "mark of the beast" still remains to be defined.

After the warning against the worship of the beast and his image, the prophecy declares, "Here are they that keep the commandments of God, and the faith of Jesus." Since those who keep God's commandments are thus placed in contrast with those that worship the beast and his image and receive his mark, it follows that the keeping of God's law, on the one hand, and its violation, on the other, will make the distinction between the worshipers of God and the worshipers of the beast.

Think to Change

The special characteristic of the beast, and therefore of his image, is the breaking of God's commandments. Says Daniel of the little horn, the papacy, "He shall think to change the times and the law" (Dan. 7:25, R.V.). And Paul styled the same power the "man of sin," who was to exalt himself above God. One prophecy is a complement of the other. Only by changing God's law could the papacy exalt itself above God; whoever should understandingly keep the law as thus changed would be giving supreme honor to that power by which the change was made. Such an act of obedience to papal laws would be a mark of allegiance to the pope in the place of God.

The papacy has attempted to change the law of God. The second commandment, forbidding image worship, has been dropped from the law, and the fourth commandment has been so changed as to authorize the observance of the first instead of the seventh day as the Sabbath. But papists urge, as a reason for omitting the second commandment, that it is unnecessary, being included in the first, and that they are giving the law exactly as God designed it to be understood. This cannot be the change foretold by the prophet. An intentional, deliberate change is presented: "He shall *think* to change the times and the law." The change in the fourth commandment exactly fulfills the prophecy. For this, the only authority claimed is that of the church. Here the papal power openly sets itself above God.

The Bible or the Papacy

While the worshipers of God will be especially distinguished by their regard for the fourth commandment,— since this is the sign of His creative power and the witness to His claim upon man's reverence and homage,—the worshipers of the beast will be distinguished by their efforts to tear down the Creator's memorial, to exalt the in-

stitution of Rome. It was in behalf of the Sunday that popery first asserted its arrogant claims; and its first resort to
the power of the State was to compel the observance of
Sunday as "the Lord's day." But the Bible points to the
seventh day, and not to the first, as the Lord's day. Said
Christ, "The Son of man is Lord also of the Sabbath." The
fourth commandment declares: "The seventh day is the
Sabbath of the Lord." And by the prophet Isaiah the Lord
designates it "My holy day" (Mark 2:28; Isa. 58:13).

The claim so often put forth, that Christ changed the
Sabbath, is disproved by His own words. It is a fact gener-
ally admitted by Protestants, that the Scriptures give no
authority for the change of the Sabbath. Roman Catholics
acknowledge that the change of the Sabbath was made by
their church, and declare that Protestants, by observing the
Sunday, are recognizing her power.

The Mark of Papal Authority

As the sign of the authority of the Catholic Church,
papist writers cite "the very act of changing the Sabbath
into Sunday, which Protestants allow of . . because by keeping Sunday strictly they acknowledge the church's power
to ordain feasts and to command them under sin" (*Abridge-
ment of Christian Doctrine, p. 58, H. Tuberville*). What
then is the change of the Sabbath, but the sign or mark of
the authority of the Romish Church—"the mark of the
beast?"

The Roman Church has not relinquished her claim to
supremacy; and when the world and the Protestant churches
accept a sabbath of her creating—while they reject the
Bible Sabbath—they virtually admit this assumption. They
may claim the authority of tradition and of the Fathers for
the change; but in so doing they ignore the very principle
which separates them from Rome,—that "the Bible, and
the Bible only, is the religion of Protestants." The papists
can see that they are deceiving themselves, willingly closing their eyes to the facts in the case. As the movement for
Sunday enforcement gains favor, he rejoices, feeling assured that it will eventually bring the whole Protestant world

ınder the banner of Rome.

Worshiping the Beast

Romanists declare that "the observance of Sunday by the Protestants is an homage they pay, in spite of themselves, to the authority of the [Catholic] Church" (*"Plain Talk About Protestantism," p. 213*). The enforcement of Sundaykeeping on the part of Protestant churches is an enforcement of the worship of the papacy—of the beast. Those who, understanding the claims of the fourth commandment, choose to observe the false instead of the true Sabbath, are thereby paying homage to that power by which alone it is commanded. But in the very act of enforcing a religious duty by secular power, the churches would themselves form an image to the beast; hence the enforcement of Sundaykeeping in the United States would be an enforcement of the worship of the beast and his image.

But Christians of past generations observed the Sunday, supposing that in so doing they were keeping the Bible Sabbath; and there are now true Christians in every church, not excepting the Roman Catholic communion, who honestly believe that Sunday is the Sabbath of divine appointment. God accepts their sincerity of purpose and their integrity before Him. But when Sunday observance shall be enforced by law, and the world shall be enlightened concerning the obligation of the true Sabbath, then whoever shall transgress the command of God, to obey a precept which has no higher authority than that of Rome, will thereby honor popery above God. He is paying homage to Rome and to the power which enforces the institution ordained by Rome. He is worshiping the beast and his image. As men then reject the institution which God has declared to be the sign of His authority, and honor in its stead that which Rome has chosen as the token of her supremacy, they will thereby accept the sign of allegiance to Rome—"the mark of the beast." And it is not until the issue is thus plainly set before the people—and they are brought to choose between the commandments of God and the commandments of men—that those who continue in transgression will receive "the mark of the beast."

The Warning against the Mark

The most fearful threatening ever addressed to mortals is contained in the third angel's message. That must be a terrible sin which calls down the wrath of God unmingled with mercy. Men are not to be left in darkness concerning this important matter; the warning against this sin is to be given to the world before the visitation of God's judgments, that all may know why they are to be inflicted, and have opportunity to escape them. Prophecy declares that the first angel would make his announcement to "every nation and kindred, and tongue, and people." The warning of the third angel, which forms a part of the same threefold message, is to be no less widespread. It is represented in the prophecy as proclaimed with a loud voice, by an angel flying in the midst of heaven; and it will command the attention of the world!

Two Great Classes

In the issue of the contest, all Christendom will be divided into two great classes,—those who keep the commandments of God and the faith of Jesus, and those who worship the beast and his image and receive his mark. Although church and State will unite their power to compel "all, both small and great, rich and poor, free and bond, to receive the mark" of the beast (Rev. 13:16), yet the people of God will not receive it. The prophet of Patmos beholds "them that had gotten the victory over the beast, and over his image, and over his mark, and over the number of his name stand on the sea of glass, having the harps of God," and singing the song of Moses and the Lamb (Rev. 15:2-3).

Protestants Are Changing

Romanism is now regarded by Protestants with far greater favor than in former years. In those countries where Catholicism is not in the ascendancy, and the papists are taking a conciliatory course in order to gain influence, there is an increasing indifference concerning the doctrines that separate the Reformed churches from the papal hierarchy; the opinion is gaining ground that, after all, we do not differ so widely upon vital points as has been supposed, and that a little concession on our part will bring us into a better understanding with Rome. The time was when Protestants placed a high value upon the liberty of conscience which has been so dearly purchased. They taught their children to abhor popery and held that to seek harmony with Rome would be disloyalty to God. But how widely different are the sentiments now expressed. The defenders of popery declare that the church has been maligned; and the Protestant world are inclined to accept the statement. Many urge that it is unjust to judge the church of today by the abominations and absurdities that marked her reign during the centuries of ignorance and darkness. They excuse her horrible cruelty as the result of the barbarism of the times, and plead that the influence of modern civilization has changed her sentiments.

Babylon Has Not Changed

Have these persons forgotten the claim of infallibility put forth for nine hundred years by this haughty power? So far from being relinquished, this claim has been affirmed in the twentieth century with greater positiveness than ever before. As Rome asserts that she *"never erred, and never can err,"* how can she renounce the principles which governed her course in past ages?

The papal church will never relinquish her claim to infallibility. All that she has done in her persecution of those who reject her dogmas, she holds to be right; and would she not repeat the same acts, should the opportunity be presented? Let the restraints now imposed by secular governments be removed, and Rome be reinstated in her former power, and there would speedily be a revival of her tyranny and persecution.

Forgetting the Past

The Roman Church now presents a fair front to the world, covering with apologies her record of horrible cruelties. She has clothed herself in Christ-like garments; bu she is unchanged. Every principle of popery that existed in past ages exists today. The doctrines devised in the dark est ages *are still held*. Let none deceive themselves. The popery that Protestants are now so ready to honor is the same that ruled the world in the days of the Reformation when men of God stood up, at the peril of their lives, to expose her iniquity. She possesses the same pride and ar rogant assumption that lorded it over kings and princes and claimed the prerogatives of God. Her spirit is no les cruel and despotic now than when she crushed out human liberty and slew the saints of the Most High.

The papacy is just what prophecy declared that she would be, the apostasy of the latter times (2 Thess. 2:3-4) It is a part of her policy to assume the character which wil best accomplish her purpose; but beneath the variable ap pearance of the chameleon, she conceals the invariable venom of the serpent. "We are not bound to keep faith and promises to heretics," she declares. Shall this power, whose record for a thousand years is written in the blood of the saints, be now acknowledged as a part of the church o Christ?

What Has Changed

It is not without reason that the claim has been pu forth in Protestant countries, that Catholicism differs les widely from Protestantism than in former times. There ha been a change; but the change is not in the papacy. Ca tholicism indeed resembles much of the Protestantism tha now exists, because Protestantism has so greatly degener ated since the days of the Reformers.

A prayerful study of the Bible would show Protestant the real character of the papacy, and would cause them to abhor and to shun it; but many are so wise in their own conceit that they feel no need of humbly seeking God tha they may be led into the truth. Although priding themselve on their enlightenment, they are ignorant both of the Scrip tures and of the power of God. They must have some mean of quieting their consciences; and they seek that which is least spiritual and humiliating. *What they desire is a method of forgetting God which shall pass as a method of remembering Him.* The papacy is well adapted to meet the wants of all these. It is prepared for two classes of mankind, embracing nearly the whole world,—those who would be saved by their merits, and those who would be saved in their sins. Here is the secret of its power.

A day of great intellectual darkness has been shown to be favorable to the success of popery. It will yet be demonstrated that a day of great intellectual light is equally favorable for its success.

Following in the Steps

In the movements now in progress in the United States to secure for the institutions and usages of the church the support of the state, Protestants are following in the steps of papists. Nay, more, they are opening the door for the papacy to regain in Protestant America the supremacy which she has lost in the Old World. And that which gives greater significance to this movement is the fact that the principal object contemplated is the enforcement of Sunday observance,—a custom which originated with Rome, and which she claims as the sign of her authority. It is the spirit of the papacy—the spirit of conformity to worldly customs, the veneration for human traditions above the commandments of God,—that is permeating the Protestant churches and leading them on to do the same work of Sunday exaltation which the papacy has done before them.

These records of the past clearly reveal the enmity of Rome toward the true Sabbath and its defenders, and the means which she employs to honor the institution of her creating.

Protestants little know what they are doing when they propose to accept the aid of Rome in the work of Sunday exaltation. While they are bent upon the accomplishment of their purpose, Rome is aiming to re-establish her power, to recover her lost supremacy. Let history testify of her artful and persistent efforts to insinuate herself into the affairs of nations; and having gained a foothold, to further

her own aims, even at the ruin of princes and people
Romanism openly puts forth the claim that the pope "can
pronounce sentences and judgments in contradiction to the
right of nations, to the law of God and man" (*The "Decre-
talia"*).

And let it be remembered: it is the boast of Rome that
she never changes. The principles of Gregory VII and Innocent III are still the principles of the Roman Church.
And had she but the power, she would put them in practice
with as much vigor now as in past centuries. Let the principle once be established in the United States, that the
church may employ or control the power of the State; that
religious observances may be enforced by secular laws; in
short, that the authority of church and State is to dominate
the conscience—and the triumph of Rome in this country
is assured.

"In all thy ways acknowledge Him, and He
shall direct thy paths."
                                              —*Proverbs 3:6*

"The blood of Jesus Christ, His Son,
cleanseth us from all sin . . If we confess
our sins, He is faithful and just to forgive
us our sins, and to cleanse us from all
unrighteousness."
                                              —*1 John 1:7, 9*

"And whatsoever we ask, we receive of
Him, because we keep His
commandments, and do those things
that are pleasing in His sight."
                                              —*1 John 3:22*

"Be thou faithful unto death, and I will give
thee a crown of Life."
                                              —*Revelation 2:10*

Chapter Four

Supernatural Power to Destroy

— Talking with Devils

One of the most fantastic deceptions of all time was started by the devil thousands of years ago. Surprisingly enough, few today recognize it for what it is. And yet with it, he catches souls and holds them fast —

You are now going to learn the heart of the spiderweb—how Satan uses the dead—to catch the living —

With the earliest history of man, Satan began his efforts to deceive our race. He who had incited rebellion in Heaven desired to bring the inhabitants of the earth to unite with him in his warfare against the government of God. Adam and Eve had been perfectly happy in obedience to the law of God, and this fact was a constant testimony against the claim which Satan had urged in Heaven, that God's law was oppressive and opposed to the good of His creatures. And, furthermore, Satan's envy was excited as he looked upon the beautiful home prepared for the sinless pair. He determined to cause their fall that, having separated them from God and brought them under his own power, he might gain possession of the earth and here establish his kingdom, in opposition to the Most High.

"The woman said unto the serpent, We may eat of the fruit of the trees of the garden: but of the fruit of the tree which is in the midst of the garden God hath said, Ye shall not eat of it, neither shall ye touch it, lest ye die. And the serpent said unto the woman, Ye shall not surely die;

for God doth know that in the day ye eat thereof, then your eyes shall be opened, and ye shall be as gods, knowing good and evil." *Genesis 3:2-5.*

Immortality by Obedience

In the midst of Eden grew the tree of life, whose fruit had the power of perpetuating life. Had Adam remained obedient to God, he would have continued to enjoy free access to this tree, and would have lived forever. But when he sinned, he was cut off from partaking of the tree of life, and he became subject to death. The divine sentence, "Dust thou art, and unto dust shalt thou return," points to the utter extinction of life.

Immortality, promised to man on condition of obedience, had been forfeited by transgression. Adam could not transmit to his posterity that which he did not possess; and there could have been no hope for the fallen race, had not God—by the sacrifice of His Son—"brought life and immortality to light through the gospel" (Rom. 5:12; 2 Tim. 1:10). And only through Christ can immortality be obtained. Said Jesus, "He that believeth on the Son hath everlasting life; and he that believeth not the Son shall not see life" (John 3:36). Every man may come in possession of this priceless blessing if he will comply with the conditions. All "who by patient continuance in well-doing seek for glory and honor and immortality" will receive eternal life (Rom. 2:7).

No Immortal Sinner

The only one who promised Adam life in disobedience was the great deceiver. And the declaration of the serpent to Eve in Eden,—"Ye shall not surely die,"—was the first sermon ever preached upon the immortality of the soul. Yet this declaration, resting solely upon the authority of Satan, is echoed from the pulpits of Christendom, and is received by the majority of mankind as readily as it was received by our first parents. The divine sentence, "The soul that sinneth, it shall die" (Eze. 18:20) is made to mean, The soul that sinneth, it shall not die, but live eternally. We cannot but wonder at the strange infatuation which renders men so credulous concerning the words of Satan, and so unbelieving in regard to the words of God.

Had man, after his fall, been allowed free access to the tree of life, he would have lived forever, and thus sin would have been immortalized. But cherubim and a flaming sword kept "the way of the tree of life" (Gen. 3:24), and not one of the family of Adam has been permitted to pass that barrier and partake of the life-giving fruit. Therefore there is not an immortal sinner.

"Ye Shall Not Surely Die"

But after the fall, Satan bade his angels make a special effort to inculcate the belief in man's natural immortality; and having induced the people to receive this error, they were to lead them on to conclude that the sinner would live in eternal misery. Now the prince of darkness, working through his agents, represents God as a revengeful tyrant, declaring that He plunges into hell all those who do not please Him, and causes them ever to feel His wrath; and that while they suffer unutterable anguish and writhe in the eternal flames, their Creator looks down upon them with satisfaction.

Misrepresenting God's Character

How repugnant to every emotion of love and mercy, and even to our sense of justice, is the doctrine that the wicked dead are tormented with fire and brimstone in an eternally burning hell; that for the sins of a brief, earthly life they are to suffer torture as long as God shall live. Yet this doctrine has been widely taught, and is still embodied in many of the creeds of Christendom. It is urged that the infliction of endless misery upon the wicked would show God's hatred of sin as an evil which is ruinous to the peace and order of the universe. Oh, dreadful blasphemy! As if God's hatred of sin is the reason why He perpetuates sin. For, according to the teachings of these theologians, continued torture without hope of mercy maddens its wretched victims, and as they pour out their rage in curses and blasphemy, they are forever augmenting their load of guilt. God's glory is not enhanced by thus perpetuating continually increasing sin through ceaseless ages.

The Opposite Error

A large class to whom the doctrine of eternal torment is revolting are driven to the opposite error. They see that the Scriptures represent God as a being of love and compassion, and they cannot believe that He will consign His creatures to the fires of an eternally burning hell. But, holding that the soul is naturally immortal, they see no alternative but to conclude that all mankind will finally be saved. Many regard the threatenings of the Bible as designed merely to frighten men into obedience, and not to be literally fulfilled. Thus the sinner can live in selfish pleasure, disregarding the requirements of God, and yet expect to be finally received into His favor. Such a doctrine, presuming upon God's mercy—but ignoring His justice—pleases the carnal heart, and emboldens the wicked in their iniquity.

The Wages of Sin Is Death

God has given in His Word decisive evidence that He will punish the transgressors of His law. Those who flatter themselves, that He is too merciful to execute justice upon the sinner, have only to look to the cross of Calvary. The death of the spotless Son of God testifies that "the wages of sin is death," that every violation of God's law must receive its just retribution. Christ the sinless became sin for man. He bore the guilt of transgression, and the hiding of His Father's face, until His heart was broken and His life crushed out. All this sacrifice was made that sinners might be redeemed. In no other way could man be freed from the penalty of sin. And every soul that refuses to become a partaker of the atonement provided at such a cost must bear, in his own person, the guilt and punishment of transgression.

"He that overcometh shall inherit all things; and I will be his God, and he shall be My son." *Revelation 21:7.* Here, also, conditions are specified. In order to inherit all things, we must resist and overcome sin.

Obedience by Faith in Christ

"No fornicator, nor unclean person, nor covetous man, who is an idolater, hath any inheritance in the kingdom of Christ and God." *Ephesians 5:5, R.V.* "Follow peace with all men, and holiness, without which no man shall see the Lord." *Hebrews 12:14.* "Blessed are they that do His commandments, that they may have right to the tree of life, and may enter in through the gates into the city. For without are dogs, and sorcerers, and whoremongers, and murderers, and idolaters, and whosoever loveth and maketh a lie." *Revelation 22:14-15.*

For the Good of All

God executes justice upon the wicked, for the good of the universe, and even for the good of those upon whom His judgments are visited. He would make them happy if He could do so in accordance with the laws of His government and the justice of His character. He surrounds them with the tokens of His love, He grants them a knowledge of His law, and follows them with the offers of His mercy; but they despise His love, make void His law, and reject His mercy.

Those who have chosen Satan as their leader, and have been controlled by his power, are not prepared to enter the presence of God. Pride, deception, licentiousness, and cruelty have become fixed in their characters. Can they enter Heaven, to dwell forever with those whom they despised and hated on earth? Truth will never be agreeable to a liar; meekness will not satisfy self-esteem and pride; purity is not acceptable to the corrupt; disinterested love does not appear attractive to the selfish. What source of enjoyment could Heaven offer to those who are wholly absorbed in earthly and selfish interests?

Life or Death

"The wages of sin is death; but the gift of God is eternal life through Jesus Christ our Lord." *Romans 6:23.*

While life is the inheritance of the righteous, death is the portion of the wicked. Moses declared to Israel: "I have set before thee this day life and good, and death and evil." *Deuteronomy 30:15*. The death referred to in these Scriptures is not that pronounced upon Adam, for all mankind suffer the penalty of his transgression. It is the "second death" that is placed in contrast with everlasting life.

In consequence of Adam's sin, death passed upon the whole human race. All alike go down into the grave. And through the provisions of the plan of salvation, all are to be brought forth from their graves. "There shall be a resurrection of the dead, both of the just and unjust." *Acts 24:15*. "For as in Adam all die, even so in Christ shall all be made alive." *1 Corinthians 15:22*.

But a distinction is made between the two classes that are brought forth. "All that are in the graves shall hear His voice, and shall come forth; they that have done good, unto the resurrection of life; and they that have done evil, unto the resurrection of damnation," *John 5:28-29*. They who have been "accounted worthy" of the resurrection of life are "blessed and holy." "On such the second death hath no power" (Rev. 20:6). But those who have not through repentance and faith secured pardon, must receive the penalty of transgression,—"the wages of sin." They suffer punishment varying in duration and intensity, "according to their works," but finally ending in the second death.

Since it is impossible for God, consistently with His justice and mercy to save the sinner in his sins, He deprives him of the existence which his transgressions have forfeited, and of which he has proved himself unworthy. Says an inspired writer, "Yet a little while, and the wicked shall not be; yea, thou shalt diligently consider his place, and it shall not be." And another declares, "They shall be as though they had not been" (Ps. 37:10; Obad. 16). Covered with infamy, they sink into hopeless, eternal oblivion.

An End of Sin

Thus will be made an end of sin, with all the woe and ruin which have resulted from it. Says the psalmist: "Thou hast destroyed the wicked, Thou hast put out their name forever and ever. O thou enemy, destructions are come to a perpetual end." *Psalm 9:5-6*. John, in the Revelation, looking forward to the eternal state, hears a universal anthem of praise undisturbed by one note of discord. Every creature in Heaven and earth was heard ascribing glory to God (Rev. 5:13). There will then be no lost souls to blaspheme God, as they writhe in never-ending torment; no wretched beings in hell will mingle their shrieks with the songs of the saved.

A Second Error

Upon the fundamental error of natural immortality rests the doctrine of consciousness in death—a doctrine, like eternal torment, opposed to the teachings of the Scriptures, to the dictates of reason, and to our feelings of humanity. According to the popular belief, the redeemed in Heaven are acquainted with all that takes place on the earth, and especially with the lives of the friends whom they have left behind. But how could it be a source of happiness to the dead to know the troubles of the living, to witness the sins committed by their own loved ones, and to see them enduring all the sorrows, disappointments, and anguish of life? How much of Heaven's bliss would be enjoyed by those who were hovering over their friends on earth? And how utterly revolting is the belief that as soon as the breath leaves the body, the soul of the impenitent is consigned to the flames of hell! To what depths of anguish must those be plunged who see their friends passing to the grave unprepared, to enter upon an eternity of woe and sin! Many have been driven to insanity by this harrowing thought.

The Bible Says

What say the Scriptures concerning these things? David declares that man is not conscious in death. "His breath goeth forth, he returneth to his earth; in that very day his thoughts perish." *Psalm 146:4*. Solomon bears the same testimony: "The living know that they shall die; but the dead know not anything." "Their love, and their hatred, and their envy, is now perished; neither have they any more a portion forever in anything that is done under the sun." "There is no work, nor device, nor knowledge, nor wisdom, in the grave, whither thou goest." *Ecclesiastes 9:5-6, 10.*

When, in answer to his prayer, Hezekiah's life was prolonged fifteen years, the grateful king rendered to God a tribute of praise for His great mercy. In this song he tells the reason why he thus rejoices: "The grave cannot praise Thee, death cannot celebrate Thee; they that go down into the pit cannot hope for Thy truth. The living, the living, he shall praise Thee, as I do this day." *Isaiah 38:18-19.* Popular theology represents the righteous dead as in Heaven, entered into bliss, and praising God with an immortal tongue; but Hezekiah could see no such glorious prospect in death. With his words agrees the testimony of the psalmist: "In death there is no remembrance of Thee; in the grave who shall give Thee thanks?" "The dead praise not the Lord, neither any that go down into silence." *Psalms 6:5; 115:17.*

And said Paul: "If the dead rise not, then is not Christ raised: and if Christ be not raised, your faith is vain; ye are yet in your sins. Then they also which are fallen asleep in Christ are perished." *1 Corinthians 15:16-18.* If for four thousand years the righteous had gone directly to Heaven at death, how could Paul have said that if there is no resurrection, "they which are fallen asleep in Christ are perished?" No resurrection would be necessary.

The Truth of the Resurrection

It is an undeniable fact that the hope of immortal blessedness at death has led to widespread neglect of the Bible doctrine of the resurrection. But when about to leave His disciples, Jesus did not tell them that they would soon come to Him. "I go to prepare a place for you," He said. "And if I go and prepare a place for you, I will come again, and receive you unto Myself." *John 14:2-3.* And Paul tells us, further, that "the Lord Himself shall descend from Heaven with a shout, with the voice of the archangel, and with the trump of God; and the dead in Christ shall rise first. Then we which are alive and remain shall be caught up together with them in the clouds, to meet the Lord in the air: and so shall we ever be with the Lord." And he adds, "Comfort one another with these words" (1 Thess. 4:16-18).

Paul points his brethren to the future coming of the Lord, when the fetters of the tomb shall be broken and the "dead in Christ" shall be raised to eternal life.

The Investigative Judgment

Before any can enter the mansions of the blest, their cases must be investigated, and their characters and their deeds must pass in review before God. All are to be judged according to the things written in the books, and to be rewarded as their works have been. This Judgment does not take place at death. Mark the words of Paul: "He hath appointed a day, in the which He will judge the world in righteousness by that man whom He hath ordained; whereof He hath given assurance unto all men, in that He hath raised Him from the dead." *Acts 17:31*. Here the apostle plainly stated that a specified time, then future, had been fixed upon for the Judgment of the world. Jude refers to the same period (Jude 14-15), and so does John in the Revelation (Rev. 20:12). But if the dead are already enjoying the bliss of Heaven or writhing in the flames of hell, what need of a future Judgment? The teachings of God's Word on these important points are neither obscure nor contradictory; they may be understood by common minds. But what candid mind can see either wisdom or justice in the current theory?

Glorious Awakening

The Bible clearly teaches that the dead do not go immediately to Heaven. They are represented as sleeping until the resurrection (1 Thess. 4:14; Job 14:10-12). In the very day when the silver cord is loosed and the golden bowl broken (Eccl. 12:6), man's thoughts perish. They that go down to the grave are in silence. They know no more of anything that is done under the sun (Job 14:21).

Blessed rest for the weary righteous! Time, be it long

or short, is but a moment to them. They sleep, they are awakened by the trump of God to a glorious immortality. "For the trumpet shall sound, and the dead shall be raised incorruptible .. So when this corruptible shall have put on incorruption, and this mortal shall have put on immortality, then shall be brought to pass the saying that is written, Death is swallowed up in victory." *1 Corinthians 15:52, 54*. As they are called forth from their deep slumber, they begin to think just where they ceased. The last sensation was the pang of death, the last thought that they were falling beneath the power of the grave. When they arise from the tomb, their first glad thought will be echoed in the triumphal shout, "O death, where is thy sting? O grave, where is thy victory" (1 Cor. 15:55)?

Preparation for Spiritualism

The doctrine of man's consciousness in death, especially the belief that the spirits of the dead return to minister to the living, has prepared the way for modern spiritualism. Here is a channel regarded as sacred, through which Satan works for the accomplishment of his purposes. The fallen angels who do his bidding appear as messengers from the spirit world. While professing to bring the living into communication with the dead, the prince of evil exercises his bewitching influence upon their minds.

Satanic Counterfeits

He has power to bring before men the appearance of their departed friends. The counterfeit is perfect; the familiar look, the words, the tone are reproduced with marvelous distinctness. Many are comforted with the assurance that their loved ones are enjoying the bliss of Heaven; and without suspicion of danger, they give ear to "seducing spirits, and doctrines of devils."

When they have been led to believe that the dead actually return to communicate with them, Satan causes those to appear who went into the grave unprepared. They claim to be happy in Heaven, and even to occupy exalted positions there; and thus the error is widely taught, that no difference is made between the righteous and the wicked. The pretended visitants from the world of spirits sometimes utter cautions and warnings which prove to be correct. Then, as confidence is gained, they present doctrines that directly undermine faith in the Scriptures.

A Supernatural Power

Many will be ensnared through the belief that spiritualism is a merely human imposture; when brought face to face with manifestations which they cannot but regard as supernatural, they will be deceived, and will be led to accept them as the great power of God.

These persons overlook the testimony of the Scriptures concerning the wonders wrought by Satan and his agents. It was by satanic aid that Pharaoh's magicians were enabled to counterfeit the work of God. Paul testifies that before the second advent of Christ there will be similar manifestations of satanic power. The coming of the Lord is to be preceded by "the working of Satan with all power and signs and lying wonders, and with all deceivableness of unrighteousness" (2 Thess. 2:9-10). No mere impostures are here foretold. Men are deceived by the miracles which Satan's agents have power to do, not which they pretend to do.

Something for Everyone

The prince of darkness, who has so long bent the powers of his mastermind to the work of deception, skillfully adapts his temptations to men of all classes and conditions. To persons of culture and refinement he presents spiritualism in its more refined and intellectual aspects, and thus succeeds in drawing many into his snare.

Satan beguiles men now as he beguiled Eve in Eden, by flattery, by kindling a desire to obtain forbidden knowledge, by exciting ambition for self-exaltation. It was cherishing these evils that caused his fall, and through them he aims to compass the ruin of men. "Ye shall be as gods," he declares, "knowing good and evil." *Genesis 3:5*. Thus, in place of the righteousness and perfection of the infinite

God, the true object of adoration—in place of the perfect righteousness of His law, the true standard of human attainment—Satan has substituted the sinful, erring nature of man himself as the only object of adoration, the only rule of judgment, or standard of character. This is progress, not upward, but downward.

To the self-indulgent, the pleasure-loving, the sensual, spiritualism presents itself under a less subtle disguise than to the more refined and intellectual; in its grosser forms they find that which is in harmony with their inclinations. When the people are thus led to believe that desire is the highest law, that liberty is license, and that man is accountable only to himself, who can wonder that corruption and depravity teem on every hand? Multitudes eagerly accept teachings that leave them at liberty to obey the promptings of the carnal heart.

None Need Be Deceived

But none need be deceived by the lying claims of spiritualism. God has given the world sufficient light to enable them to discover the snare. As already shown, the theory which forms the very foundation of spiritualism is at war with the plainest statements of Scripture. The Bible declares that the dead know not anything, that their thoughts have perished; they have no part in anything that is done under the sun; they know nothing of the joys or sorrows of those who were dearest to them on earth.

Furthermore, God has expressly forbidden all pretended communication with departed spirits. In the days of the Hebrews there was a class of people who claimed—as do the spiritualists of today—to hold communication with the dead. But the "familiar spirits" (as these visitants from other worlds were called), are declared by the Bible to be the "spirits of devils." (Compare Num. 25:1-3; Ps. 106:28; 1 Cor. 10:20; Rev. 16:14.) The work of dealing with familiar spirits was pronounced an abomination to the Lord, and was solemnly forbidden under penalty of death (Lev. 19:31; 20:27).

The very name of witchcraft is now held in contempt.

The claim that men can hold intercourse with evil spirits is regarded as a fable of the Dark Ages. But spiritualism, which numbers its converts by hundreds of thousands, yea, by millions—which has made its way into scientific circles, which has invaded churches, and has found favor in legislative bodies, and even in the courts of kings—this mammoth deception is but a revival, in a new guise, of the witchcraft condemned and prohibited of old. If there were no other evidence of the real character of spiritualism, it should be enough for the Christian that the spirits make no difference between righteousness and sin, between the noblest and purest of the apostles of Christ and the most corrupt of the servants of Satan.

A Terrible Power

There are few who have any just conception of the deceptive power of spiritualism and the danger of coming under its influence. Many tamper with it merely to gratify their curiosity. They have no real faith in it, and would be filled with horror at the thought of yielding themselves to the spirits' control. But they venture upon the forbidden ground, and the mighty destroyer exercises his power upon them against their will. Let them once be induced to submit their minds to his direction, and he holds them captive. It is impossible in their own strength to break away from the bewitching, alluring spell. Nothing but the power of God, granted in answer to the earnest prayer of faith, can deliver these ensnared souls.

Delusion by Choice

Says the prophet Isaiah: "When they shall say unto you, Seek unto them that have familiar spirits, and unto wizards that peep, and that mutter: should not a people seek unto their God? for the living to the dead? To the law and to the testimony: If they speak not according to this Word, it is because there is no light in them." *Isaiah 8:19-20*. If men had been willing to receive the truth so plainly stated in the Scriptures concerning the nature of man and the state of the dead, they would see in the claims and manifestations of spiritualism the working of Satan with power and signs and lying wonders. But rather than yield the liberty so agreeable to the carnal heart and renounce the sins which they love, multitudes close their eyes to the light and walk straight on, regardless of warnings while Satan weaves his snares about them, and they become his prey. "Because they received not the love of the truth, that they might be saved"; therefore "God shall send them strong delusion, that they should believe a lie" (2 Thess. 2:10-11). Those who would stand in this time of peril must understand for themselves the testimony of the Scriptures.

Know Your Bible

Many will be confronted by the spirits of devils personating beloved relatives or friends, and declaring the most dangerous heresies. These visitants will appeal to our tenderest sympathies, and will work miracles to sustain their pretensions. We must be prepared to withstand them with the Bible truth that the dead know not anything, and that they who thus appear are the spirits of devils.

The Hour of Temptation

Just before us is the "hour of temptation, which shall come upon all the world, to try them that dwell upon the earth" (Rev. 3:10). All whose faith is not firmly established upon the Word of God will be deceived and overcome. Satan "works with all deceivableness of unrighteousness" to gain control of the children of men; and his deceptions will continually increase. But he can gain his object only as men voluntarily yield to his temptations. Those who are earnestly seeking a knowledge of the truth, and are striving to purify their souls through obedience, thus doing what they can to prepare for the conflict will find, in the God of truth, a sure defense. "Because thou hast kept the word of My patience, I also will keep thee" (Rev. 3:10) is the Saviour's promise. He would sooner send every angel out of Heaven to protect His people, than leave one soul that trusts in Him to be overcome by Satan.

A Covenant with Death

The prophet Isaiah brings to view the fearful deception which will come upon the wicked, causing them to count themselves secure from the judgments of God: "We have made a covenant with death, and with hell are we at agreement; when the overflowing scourge shall pass through, it shall not come unto us; for we have made lies our refuge, and under falsehood have we hid ourselves." *Isaiah 28:15.*

Satan's Masterpiece

Satan has long been preparing for his final effort to deceive the world. The foundation of his work was laid by the assurance given to Eve in Eden, "Ye shall not surely die." "In the day ye eat thereof, then your eyes shall be opened, and ye shall be as gods, knowing good and evil." *Genesis 3:4-5.* Little by little he has prepared the way for his masterpiece of deception in the development of spiritualism. He has not yet reached the full accomplishment of his designs; but it will be reached in the last remnant of time. Says the prophet: "I saw three unclean spirits like frogs . . they are the spirits of devils, working miracles, which go forth unto the kings of the earth and of the whole world, to gather them to the battle of that great day of God Almighty." *Revelation 16:13-14.* Except those who are kept by the power of God through faith in His Word, the whole world will be swept into the ranks of this delusion. The people are fast being lulled to a fatal security, to be awakened only by the outpouring of the wrath of God.

Saith the Lord God: "Judgment also will I lay to the line, and righteousness to the plummet; and the hail shall sweep away the refuge of lies, and the waters shall overflow the hiding place. And your covenant with death shall be disannulled, and your agreement with hell shall not stand; when the overflowing scourge shall pass through, then ye shall be trodden down by it." *Isaiah 28:17-18.*

Chapter Five

Entering the Final Crisis

— By Threat or by Violence

Satan's power to deceive can be very great—when men choose to remain ignorant. **In every age there has been a decided struggle of truth against error. But the greatest one is just ahead. One of the most massive crises of the ages is just before mankind.** Of Babylon at this time, it is declared in Scripture, "Her sins have reached unto Heaven, and God hath remembered her iniquities."

Revelation 13 predicts that a time is just before us when those who honor fundamental Bible truths will be denounced as enemies of law and order. We must individually know the Word of God for ourselves, that we may stand on the right side in that day —

From the very beginning of the great controversy in Heaven it has been Satan's purpose to overthrow the law of God. It was to accomplish this that he entered upon his rebellion against the Creator; and though he was cast out of Heaven, he has continued the same warfare upon the earth. To deceive men, and thus lead them to transgress God's law, is the object which he has steadfastly pursued. Whether this be accomplished by casting aside the law altogether or by rejecting one of its precepts, the result will be ultimately the same. He that offends "in one point" manifests contempt for the whole law; his influence and example are on the side of transgression; he becomes "guilty of all" (James 2:10).

In seeking to cast contempt upon the divine statutes, Satan has perverted the doctrines of the Bible, and errors ave thus become incorporated into the faith of thousands who profess to believe the Scriptures. The last great conflict between truth and error is but the final struggle of the long-standing controversy concerning the law of God. Upon his battle we are now entering,—a battle between the laws of men and the precepts of God, between the religion of the Bible and the religion of fable and tradition.

No Error More Bold

No error accepted by the Christian world strikes more boldly against the authority of Heaven, none is more directly opposed to the dictates of reason, none is more pernicious in its results, than the modern doctrine so rapidly gaining ground that God's law is no longer binding upon men. Every nation has its laws, which command respect and obedience; no government could exist without them; and can it be conceived that the Creator of the heavens and the earth has no law to govern the beings He has made? Suppose that prominent ministers were publicly to teach that the statutes which govern their land and protect the rights of its citizens were not obligatory,—that they restricted the liberties of the people, and therefore ought not to be obeyed; how long would such men be tolerated in the pulpit? But is it a graver offense to disregard the laws of States and nations than to trample upon those divine precepts which are the foundation of all government?

It would be far more consistent for nations to abolish their statutes, and permit the people to do as they please, than for the Ruler of the universe to annul His law and leave the world without a standard to condemn the guilty or justify the obedient. Would we know the result of making void the law of God? The experiment has been tried. Terrible were the scenes enacted in France when atheism became the controlling power. It was then demonstrated to the world that to throw off the restraints which God has imposed is to accept the rule of the cruelest of tyrants. When the standard of righteousness is set aside, the way is open for the prince of evil to establish his power in the earth.

What Lawlessness Will Bring

Wherever the divine precepts are rejected, sin cease to appear sinful, or righteousness desirable. Those who refuse to submit to the government of God are wholly unfitted to govern themselves. Through their pernicious teachings, the spirit of insubordination is implanted in the heart of children and youth, who are naturally impatient of control; and a lawless, licentious state of society results. While scoffing at the credulity of those who obey the requirements of God, the multitudes eagerly accept the delusion of Satan. They give the rein to lust, and practice the sin which have called down judgments upon the heathen.

Those who teach the people to lightly regard the commandments of God sow disobedience, to reap disobedience. Let the restraint imposed by the divine law be wholly cast aside, and human laws would soon be disregarded. Because God forbids dishonest practices—coveting, lying, and defrauding—men are ready to trample upon His statutes as a hindrance to their worldly prosperity; but the results of banishing these precepts would be such as they do not anticipate. If the law were not binding, why should any fear to transgress? Property would no longer be safe. Men would obtain their neighbor's possessions by violence; and the strongest would become richest. Life itself would not be respected. The marriage vow would no longer stand as a sacred bulwark to protect the family. He who had the power would, if he desired, take his neighbor's wife by violence. The fifth commandment would be set aside with the fourth. Children would not shrink from taking the life of their parents, if by so doing they could obtain the desire of their corrupt hearts. The civilized world would become a horde of robbers and assassins; and peace, rest, and happiness would be banished from the earth.

And it Is Already Happening

Already the doctrine that men are released from obedience to God's requirements has weakened the force of moral obligation and opened the floodgates of iniquity upon the world. Lawlessness, dissipation, and corruption ar weeping in upon us like an overwhelming tide. In the family Satan is at work. His banner waves, even in professedly Christian households. There is envy, evil surmising, hypocrisy, estrangement, emulation, strife, betrayal of sacred trusts, indulgence of lust. The whole system of religious principles and doctrines which should form the foundation and framework of social life seems to be a tottering mass, ready to fall to ruin.

The Last Great Delusion

"To the law and to the testimony: If they speak not according to this Word, it is because there is no light in them." *Isaiah 8:20.* The people of God are directed to the scriptures as their safe-guard against the influence of false teachers and the delusive power of spirits of darkness. Satan employs every possible device to prevent men from obtaining a knowledge of the Bible; for its plain utterances reveal his deceptions. At every revival of God's work, the prince of evil is aroused to more intense activity; he is now putting forth his utmost efforts for a final struggle against Christ and His followers. The last great delusion is soon to open before us. Antichrist is to perform his marvelous works in our sight. So closely will the counterfeit resemble the true, that it will be impossible to distinguish between them except by the Holy Scriptures. By their testimony every statement and every miracle must be tested.

Those who endeavor to obey all the commandments of God will be opposed and derided. They can stand only in God. In order to endure the trial before them, they must understand the will of God as revealed in His Word; they can honor Him only as they have a right conception of His character, government, and purposes, and act in accordance with them. None but those who have fortified the mind with the truths of the Bible will stand through the last great conflict. To every soul will come the searching test, Shall I obey God rather than men? The decisive hour is even now at hand. Are our feet planted on the rock of God's immutable Word? Are we prepared to stand firm in defense of the commandments of God and the faith of Jesus?

Counterfeit before the Genuine

Before the final visitation of God's judgments upo the earth, there will be, among the people of the Lord, suc a revival of primitive godliness as has not been witnesse since apostolic times. The Spirit and power of God will b poured out upon His children. At that time many will sepa rate themselves from those churches in which the love o this world has supplanted love for God and His Word. Man both of ministers and people, will gladly accept those grea truths which God has caused to be proclaimed at this tim to prepare a people for the Lord's second coming. Th enemy of souls desires to hinder this work; and before th time for such a movement shall come, he will endeavor t prevent it by introducing a counterfeit. In those churche which he can bring under his deceptive power, he will mak it appear that God's special blessing is poured out; ther will be manifest what is thought to be great religious inter est. Multitudes will exult that God is working marvelousl for them, when the work is that of another spirit. Under religious guise, Satan will seek to extend his influence ove the Christian world.

In many of the revivals which have occurred durin the last half century, the same influences have been at worl to a greater or less degree, that will be manifest in th more extensive movements of the future. There is an emo tional excitement, a mingling of the true with the false, tha is well adapted to mislead. Yet none need be deceived. I the light of God's Word it is not difficult to determine th nature of these movements. Wherever men neglect th testimony of the Bible, turning away from those plain, soul testing truths which require self-denial and renunciation o the world, there we may be sure that God's blessing is nc bestowed. And by the rule which Christ Himself has giver "Ye shall know them by their fruits" (Matt. 7:16), it is ev dence that these movements are not the work of the Spir of God.

False Revivals and the True

In the truths of His Word, God has given to men

revelation of Himself; and to all who accept them they are a shield against the deceptions of Satan. It is a neglect of these truths that has opened the door to the evils which are now becoming so widespread in the religious world. The nature and the importance of the law of God have been, to a great extent, lost sight of. A wrong conception of the character, the perpetuity, and obligation of the divine law has led to errors in relation to conversion and sanctification, and has resulted in lowering the standard of piety in the church. Here is to be found the secret of the lack of the Spirit and power of God in the revivals of our time.

And then the great deceiver will persuade men that those who serve God are causing these evils. The class that have provoked the displeasure of Heaven will charge all their troubles upon those whose obedience to God's commandments is a perpetual reproof to transgressors. It will be declared that men are offending God by the violation of the Sunday-sabbath, that this sin has brought calamities which will not cease until Sunday observance shall be strictly enforced, and that those who present the claims of the fourth commandment—thus destroying reverence for Sunday—are troublers of the people, preventing their restoration to divine favor and temporal prosperity.

Double Deception

Satan's policy in this final conflict with God's people is the same that he employed in the opening of the great controversy in Heaven. He professed to be seeking to promote the stability of the divine government while secretly bending every effort to secure its overthrow. And the very work which he was thus endeavoring to accomplish he charged upon the loyal angels. The same policy of deception has marked the history of the Roman Church. It has professed to act as the vicegerent of Heaven while seeking to exalt itself above God and to change His law. While Satan seeks to destroy those who honor God's law, he will cause them to be accused as law-breakers, as men who are dishonoring God and bringing judgments upon the world.

Religious Law, the Key

God never forces the will or the conscience; bu
Satan's constant resort—to gain control of those whom h
cannot otherwise seduce—is compulsion by cruelty
Through fear or force he endeavors to rule the conscienc
and to secure homage to himself. To accomplish this, h
works through both religious and secular authorities, mov
ing them to the enforcement of human laws in defiance o
the law of God.

Those who honor the Bible Sabbath will be denounce
as enemies of law and order, as breaking down the mora
restraints of society, causing anarchy and corruption, an
calling down the judgments of God upon the earth. Thei
conscientious scruples will be pronounced obstinacy, stub
bornness, and contempt of authority. They will be accuse
of disaffection toward the government. Ministers who den
the obligation of the divine law will present from the pulpi
the duty of yielding obedience to the civil authorities a
ordained of God. In legislative halls and courts of justice
commandment keepers will be misrepresented and con
demned. A false coloring will be given to their words; th
worst construction will be put upon their motives.

Enacting a Law

As the Protestant churches reject the clear, scrip
tural arguments in defense of God's law, they will long t
silence those whose faith they cannot overthrow by th
Bible. Though they blind their own eyes to the fact, the
are now adopting a course which will lead to the persecu
tion of those who conscientiously refuse to do what th
rest of the Christian world are doing, and acknowledge th
claims of the papal sabbath. The dignitaries of church an
state will unite to bribe, persuade, or compel all classes t
honor the Sunday. The lack of divine authority will be sup
plied by oppressive enactments. Political corruption is de
stroying love of justice and regard for truth; and even i
free America, rulers and legislators, in order to secure publi
favor, will yield to the popular demand for a law enforcin
Sunday observance. Liberty of conscience, which has cos

so great a sacrifice, will no longer be respected. In the soon-coming conflict we shall see exemplified the prophet's words: "The dragon was wroth with the woman, and went to make war with the remnant of her seed, which keep the commandments of God, and have the testimony of Jesus Christ" (Rev. 12:17).

Marvelous in her shrewdness and cunning is the Roman Church. She can read what is to be. She bides her time, seeing that the Protestant churches are paying her homage in their acceptance of the false Sabbath, and that they are preparing to enforce it by the very means which she herself employed in bygone days. Those who reject the light of truth will yet seek the aid of this self-styled infallible power to exalt an institution that originated with her. How readily she will come to the help of Protestants in this work it is not difficult to conjecture. Who understands better than the papal leaders how to deal with those who are disobedient to the church?

Preparing for the End

The Roman Church, with all its ramifications throughout the world, forms one vast organization under the control, and designed to serve the interests, of the papal see. Its millions of communicants, in every country on the globe, are instructed to hold themselves as bound in allegiance to the pope. Whatever their nationality or their government, they are to regard the authority of the church as above all other. Though they may take the oath pledging their loyalty to the state, yet back of this lies the vow of obedience to Rome, absolving them from every pledge inimical to her interests.

The Warning Has Been Given

God's Word has given warning of the impending danger; let this be unheeded, and the Protestant world will learn what the purposes of Rome really are, only when it is too late to escape the snare. She is silently growing into power. Her doctrines are exerting their influence in legislative halls, in the churches, and in the hearts of men. She is piling up her lofty and massive structures, in the secret recesses of which her former persecutions will be repeated. Stealthily and unsuspectedly she is strengthening her forces to further her own ends when the time shall come for her to strike. All that she desires is vantage ground, and this is already being given her. We shall soon see and shall feel what the purpose of the Roman element is. Whoever shall believe and obey the Word of God will thereby incur reproach and persecution.

To Destroy Faith in the Bible

The iniquity and spiritual darkness that prevailed under the supremacy of Rome were the inevitable result of her suppression of the Scriptures; but where is to be found the cause of the widespread infidelity, the rejection of the law of God, and the consequent corruption, under the full blaze of gospel light in an age of religious freedom? Now that Satan can no longer keep the world under his control by withholding the Scriptures, he resorts to other means to accomplish the same object. To destroy faith in the Bible serves his purpose as well as to destroy the Bible itself. By introducing the belief that God's law is not binding, he as effectually leads men to transgress as if they were wholly ignorant of its precepts. And now, as in former ages, he has worked through the church to further his designs.

The religious organizations of the day have refused to listen to unpopular truths plainly brought to view in the Scriptures; and, in combating them, they have adopted interpretations and taken positions which have sown broadcast the seeds of skepticism. Clinging to the papal error of natural immortality and man's consciousness in death, they have rejected the only defense against the delusions of spiritualism. The doctrine of eternal torment has led many to disbelieve the Bible. And as the claims of the fourth commandment are urged upon the people, it is found that the observance of the seventh-day Sabbath is enjoined; and as the only way to free themselves from a duty which they are unwilling to perform, popular teachers declare that the law of God is no longer binding. Thus they cast away the law and the Sabbath together. As the work of Sabbath reform extends, this rejection of the divine law to avoid the claims of the fourth commandment will become almost universal. The teachings of religious leaders have opened the door to infidelity, to spiritualism, and to contempt for God's holy law; and upon these leaders rests a fearful responsibility for the iniquity that exists in the Christian world.

Two Great Errors

Through the two great errors, the immortality of the soul and Sunday sacredness, Satan will bring the people under his deceptions. While the former lays the foundation of spiritualism, the latter creates a bond of sympathy with Rome. The Protestants of the United States will be foremost in stretching their hands across the gulf to grasp the hand of spiritualism; they will reach over the abyss to clasp hands with the Roman power; and under the influence of this threefold union, this country will follow in the steps of Rome in trampling on the rights of conscience.

The Basis of Genuine Revival

Many religious teachers assert that Christ by His death abolished the law, and men are henceforth free from its requirements. There are some who represent it as a grievous yoke; and, in contrast to the bondage of the law, they present the liberty to be enjoyed under the gospel.

But not so did prophets and apostles regard the holy law of God. Said David, "I will walk at liberty; for I seek Thy precepts" (Ps. 119:45). The apostle James, who wrote after the death of Christ, refers to the decalogue as the "royal law," and the "perfect law of liberty" (James 2:8; 1:25). And the Revelator, half a century after the crucifixion, pronounces a blessing upon those "that do His commandments, that they may have right to the tree of life, and may enter in through the gates into the city" (Rev. 22:14).

The claim that Christ, by His death, abolished His Father's law is without foundation. Had it been possible for the law to be changed or set aside, then Christ need not have died to save man from the penalty of sin. The death of Christ, so far from abolishing the law, proves that it is immutable. The Son of God came to "magnify the law and make it honorable" (Isa. 42:21). He said, "Think not that I am come to destroy the law"; "till heaven and earth pass, one jot or one tittle shall in nowise pass from the law" (Matt. 5:17-18). And concerning Himself He declares, "I delight to do Thy will, O My God; yea, Thy law is within My heart" (Ps. 40:8).

The First Step in Reconciliation

The first step in reconciliation to God is the conviction of sin. "Sin is the transgression of the law." "By the law is the knowledge of sin." *1 John 3:4; Romans 3:20.* In order to see his guilt, the sinner must test his character by God's great standard of righteousness. It is a mirror which shows the perfection of a righteous character and enables him to discern the defects in his own.

The law reveals to man his sins, but it provides no remedy. While it promises life to the obedient, it declares that death is the portion of the transgressor. The gospel of Christ alone can free him from the condemnation or the defilement of sin. He must exercise repentance toward God, whose law has been transgressed and faith in Christ, his atoning sacrifice. Thus he obtains "remission of sins that are past," and becomes a partaker of the divine nature. He is a child of God, having received the spirit of adoption, whereby he cries, "Abba, Father!"

Free to Obey

Is he now free to transgress God's law? Says Paul: "Do we then make void the law through faith? God forbid; yea, we establish the law." "How shall we, that are dead to sin live any longer therein?" And John declares, "This is the love of God, that we keep His commandments: and His commandments are not grievous" (Rom. 3:31; 6:2; 1 John 5:3). In the new birth the heart is brought into harmony with God, as it is brought into accord with His law.

Satanic Delusions

As spiritualism more closely imitates the nominal

Christianity of the day, it has greater power to deceive and ensnare. Satan himself is converted after the modern order of things. He will appear in the character of an angel of light. Through the agency of spiritualism, miracles will be wrought, the sick will be healed, and many undeniable wonders will be performed. And as the spirits will profess faith in the Bible and manifest respect for the institutions of the church, their work will be accepted as a manifestation of divine power.

How Satan Will Appear

Through spiritualism, Satan appears as a benefactor of the race, healing the diseases of the people, and professing to present a new and more exalted system of religious faith; but at the same time he works as a destroyer. His temptations are leading multitudes to ruin. Intemperance dethrones reason; sensual indulgence, strife, and bloodshed follow.

The prophecy of Revelation 13 declares that the power represented by the beast with lamb-like horns shall cause "the earth and them which dwell therein" to worship the papacy—there symbolized by the beast "like unto a leopard." The beast with two horns is also to say "to them that dwell on the earth, that they should make an image to the beast"; and furthermore, it is to command all, "both small and great, rich and poor, free and bond," to receive "the mark of the beast" (Rev. 13:12, 2, 14, 16-17).

A Restoration of Her Power

And prophecy foretells a restoration of her power. "I saw one of his heads as it were wounded to death; and his deadly wound was healed; and all the world wondered after the beast." *Revelation 13:3.* The infliction of the deadly wound points to the abolition of the papacy in 1798. After this, says the prophet, "His deadly wound was healed; and all the world wondered after the beast." Paul states plainly that the man of sin will continue until the second advent (2 Thess. 2:8). To the very close of time he will carry forward his work of deception. And the Revelator declares, also referring to the papacy, "All that dwell upon the earth shall worship him, whose names are not written in the book of life" (Rev. 13:8). In both the Old and the New World, the papacy will receive homage in the honor paid to the Sunday institution, that rests solely upon the authority of the Roman Church.

Rapidly Being Fulfilled

In the events now taking place is seen a rapid advance toward the fulfillment of the prediction. With Protestant teachers there is the same claim of divine authority for Sundaykeeping, and the same lack of scriptural evidence, as with the papist leaders who fabricated miracles to supply the place of a command from God. The assertion that God's judgments are visited upon men for their violation of the Sunday-sabbath will be repeated; already it is beginning to be urged. And a movement to enforce Sunday observance is fast gaining ground.

Come Out of Her, My People

"I saw another angel come down from Heaven, having great power; and the earth was lightened with his glory. And he cried mightily with a strong voice, saying, Babylon the great is fallen, is fallen, and is become the habitation of devils, and the hold of every foul spirit, and a cage of every unclean and hateful bird." "And I heard another voice from Heaven, saying, Come out of her, My people, that ye be not partakers of her sins, and that ye receive not of her plagues." *Revelation 18:1, 2, 4.*

This Scripture points forward to a time when the announcement of the fall of Babylon, as made by the second angel of Revelation 14:8, is to be repeated, with the additional mention of the corruptions which have been entering the various organizations that constitute Babylon, since that message was first given, in the summer of 1844. A terrible condition of the religious world is here described. With every rejection of truth, the minds of the people will become darker, their hearts more stubborn, until they are entrenched in an infidel hardihood. In defiance of the warnings which

God has given, they will continue to trample upon one of the precepts of the decalogue, until they are led to persecute those who hold it sacred.

Christ is set at naught in the contempt placed upon His Word and His people. As the teachings of spiritualism are accepted by the churches, the restraint imposed upon the carnal heart is removed and the profession of religion will become a cloak to conceal the basest iniquity. A belief in spiritual manifestations opens the door to seducing spirits and doctrines of devils, and thus the influence of evil angels will be felt in the churches.

The Final Warning

Of Babylon, at the time brought to view in this prophecy, it is declared, "Her sins have reached unto heaven, and God hath remembered her iniquities" (Rev. 18:5). She has filled up the measure of her guilt, and destruction is about to fall upon her. But God still has a people in Babylon; and before the visitation of His judgments, these faithful ones must be called out, that they "partake not of her sins, and receive not of her plagues." Hence the movement symbolized by the angel coming down from Heaven, lightening the earth with his glory, and crying mightily with a strong voice, announcing the sins of Babylon. In connection with his message the call is heard, "Come out of her, My people." These announcements, uniting with the third angel's message, constitute the final warning to be given to the inhabitants of the earth.

A Clear-cut Issue

Fearful is the issue to which the world is to be brought. The powers of earth, uniting to war against the commandments of God, will decree that all, "both small and great, rich and poor, free and bond" (Rev. 13:16), shall conform to the customs of the church by the observance of the false sabbath. All who refuse compliance will be visited with civil penalties, and it will finally be declared that they are deserving of death. On the other hand, the law of God enjoining the Creator's rest day demands obedience, and threatens wrath against all who transgress its precepts.

With the issue thus clearly brought before him, whoever shall trample upon God's law to obey a human enact-
ment, receives the mark of the beast; he accepts the sign
of allegiance to the power which he chooses to obey instead of God. The warning from Heaven is, "If any man
worship the beast and his image, and receive his mark in
his forehead, or in his hand, the same shall drink of the
wine of the wrath of God, which is poured out without
mixture into the cup of His indignation" (Rev. 14:9-10).

A Clear-cut Test

The Sabbath will be the great test of loyalty; for it is
the point of truth especially controverted. When the final
test shall be brought to bear upon men, then the line of
distinction will be drawn between those who serve God
and those who serve Him not. While the observance of the
false sabbath in compliance with the law of the State, contrary to the fourth commandment, will be an avowal of
allegiance to a power that is in opposition to God; the keeping of the true Sabbath, in obedience to God's law, is an
evidence of loyalty to the Creator. While one class, by accepting the sign of submission to earthly powers receive
the mark of the beast, the other, choosing the token of allegiance to divine authority, receive the seal of God.

——— The Later Return of Christ ———

A retinue of holy angels, with bright, glittering crowns
upon their heads, escorted Him on His way. No language
can describe the glory of the scene. The living cloud of
majesty and unsurpassed glory came still nearer, and we
could clearly behold the lovely person of Jesus. He did not
wear a crown of thorns, but a crown of glory rested upon
His holy brow. Upon His vesture and thigh was a name
written, King of kings and Lord of lords. His countenance
was as bright as the noonday sun, His eyes were as a
flame of fire, and His feet had the appearance of fine brass.
His voice sounded like many musical instruments. The earth
trembled before Him, the heavens departed as a scroll when

it is rolled together, and every mountain and island were moved out of their places . . Those who a short time before would have destroyed God's faithful children from the earth, now witnessed the glory of God which rested upon them. And amid all their terror they heard the voices of the saints in joyful strains, saying, 'Lo, this is our God; we have waited for Him, and He will save us.'

The earth mightily shook as the voice of the Son of God called forth the sleeping saints. They responded to the call and came forth clothed with glorious immortality, crying, 'Victory, victory, over death and the grave! O death, where is thy sting? O grave, where is thy victory?' Then the living saints and the risen ones raised their voices in a long, transporting shout of victory. Those bodies that had gone down into the grave bearing the marks of disease and death came up in immortal health and vigor. The living saints are changed in a moment, in the twinkling of an eye, and caught up with the risen ones, and together they meet their Lord in the air. Oh, what a glorious meeting! Friends whom death had separated were united, never more to part [Early Writings, 286-287].

Friends long separated by death are united, nevermore to part, and with songs of gladness ascend together to the City of God.

——— *Life in the Earth Made New* ———

In the City of God 'there shall be no night.' None will need or desire repose. There will be no weariness in doing the will of God and offering praise to His name. We shall ever feel the freshness of the morning and shall ever be far from its close . . There, immortal minds will contemplate with never-failing delight the wonders of creative power, the mysteries of redeeming love. There will be no cruel, deceiving foe to tempt to forgetfulness of God. Every faculty will be developed, every capacity increased. The acquirement of knowledge will not weary the mind or exhaust the energies. There the grandest enterprises may be carried forward, the loftiest aspirations reached, the highest ambitions realized; and still there will arise new heights to surmount, new wonders to admire, new truths to comprehend, fresh objects to call forth the powers of mind and soul and body.

All the treasures of the universe will be open to the study of God's redeemed. Unfettered by mortality, they wing their tireless flight to worlds afar—worlds that thrilled with sorrow at the spectacle of human woe and rang with songs of gladness at the tidings of a ransomed soul. With unutterable delight the children of earth enter into the joy and the wisdom of unfallen beings. They share the treasures of knowledge and understanding gained through ages upon ages in contemplation of God's handiwork. With undimmed vision they gaze upon the glory of creation—suns and stars and systems, all in their appointed order circling the throne of Deity. Upon all things, from the least to the greatest, the Creator's name is written, and in all are the riches of His power displayed.

And the years of eternity, as they roll, will bring richer and still more glorious revelations of God and of Christ. As knowledge is progressive, so will love, reverence, and happiness increase. The more men learn of God, the greater will be their admiration of His character . . The great controversy is ended. Sin and sinners are no more. The entire universe is clean. One pulse of harmony and gladness beats through the vast creation. From Him who created all, flow life and light and gladness throughout the realms of illimitable space. From the minutest atom to the greatest world, all things, animate and inanimate, in their unshadowed beauty and perfect joy, declare that God is love.

Chapter Six

Discovering a Deeper Worship
— Going Deeper into the Word of God

In this book, we have learned that many gems of truths were lost in the Dark Ages, which we must recover today. One of the most precious is the fact that you can have a far closer walk with God than you imagined possible.

When we study God's Word—the Holy Bible—and obey its truths, we are able to enter upon the path of obedience that God invites us to enter.

In this chapter you will discover what the Scriptures say about a special truth that God has for you —

FACT NUMBER ONE—The Sabbath was given to all mankind at the Creation of this world.

The seventh-day Sabbath was given to mankind on the seventh day of Creation Week.

"Thus the heavens and the earth were finished, and all the host of them. And on the seventh day God ended His work which He had made; and he rested on the seventh day from all His work which He had made.

"And God blessed the seventh day, and sanctified it: because that in it He had rested from all His work which God created and made."—*Genesis 2:1-3.*

God dedicated and set aside the Sabbath as a rest day—2,000 years before the first Jew. Abraham is considered by all to have been the first Jew. He lived about 2000 B.C. Biblical records indicate that the Creation of this world took place about 4000 B.C. So the Bible Sabbath is not Jewish! It is for mankind; it is for all the world.

"The Sabbath was made for man."—*Mark 2:27.*

FACT NUMBER TWO—The Sabbath is a memorial of Creation and our salvation.

First, it is a memorial of Creation.

"It is a sign between Me and the children of Israel for ever: for in six days the Lord made heaven and earth, and on the seventh day He rested, and was refreshed."—*Exodus 31:17.*

As a memorial of the Creation of this world, the Sabbath cannot pass away without first having this world pass away—and creating a new one! Our planet could not have a new or different Sabbath day, without having it first hurled into oblivion—and then a new planet created from nothing. But no such event has occurred.

Second, the Sabbath is a symbol of our salvation. When we keep it, we tell all the world that we belong to God and that we serve and obey Him. The seventh-day Sabbath is a sign of our conversion, sanctification, and salvation:

"Verily My Sabbaths ye shall keep: for it is a sign between Me and you throughout your generations; that ye may know that I am the Lord that doth sanctify you."—*Exodus 31:13.*

"Moreover also I gave them My Sabbaths to be a sign between Me and them, that they might know that I am the Lord that sanctify them."—*Ezekiel 20:12.*

"And hallow My Sabbaths; and they shall be a sign between Me and you, that ye may know that I am the Lord your God."—*Ezekiel 20:20.*

But what about Christ's resurrection? Nowhere in Scripture were we told to keep any day in honor of Christ's resurrection. To do so is unscriptural. On the contrary, to set aside the Creation and sanctification Sabbath of the Bible—for another day of the week—and excuse it by saying that we do so "in honor of Christ's resurrection"—is indeed to do a very daring thing. Who dare presume to set aside the Memorial of Creation and salvation for any reason! To knowingly do so flies in the face of repeated, direct, Biblical commands by the God of heaven. To do so denies that He is our Creator and Redeemer.

If we abandon the Bible Sabbath and keep another day holy, in the

Judgment what excuse can we offer? There is no Bible reason for keeping the first day of the week holy instead of the seventh day.

FACT NUMBER THREE—**The people of God kept the Bible Sabbath before the Ten Commandments were given at Mount Sinai.**

The Sabbath Truth was first given to our race in Eden before the fall of man. It was given before sin existed, and apart from it. It was given to every man to link him to his God. And if Adam needed the Sabbath, we need it all the more today.

God's people had it before Mount Sinai. Four chapters before the Ten Commandments were given on Mount Sinai, the God of heaven spoke in such a way that it is obvious that the seventh-day Sabbath was already well-known by the people of God—but not always well-kept. Read Exodus 16.

There are those who say that the seventh-day Sabbath was not commanded by God, nor kept by man before it was spoken from Mount Sinai in Exodus 20. But Genesis 2:1-3 and Exodus 16 prove otherwise.

FACT NUMBER FOUR—**The seventh-day Sabbath Commandment lies in the very heart of the Moral Law of Ten Commandments.**

"Remember The Sabbath day, to keep it holy.

"Six days shalt thou labour, and do all thy work. But the seventh day is the Sabbath of the Lord thy God: in it thou shalt not do any work, thou, nor thy son, nor thy daughter, thy manservant, nor thy maidservant, nor thy cattle, nor thy stranger that is within thy gates.

"For in six days the Lord made heaven and earth, the sea, and all that in them is, and rested the seventh day: wherefore the Lord blessed the Sabbath day, and hallowed it."—*Exodus 20:8-11.*

The Sabbath Commandment is part of the Moral Law of Ten Commandments. The Apostle James tells us that if we break any part of this law, we have broken it all (James 2:10-12). We cannot tear out the Fourth Commandment without setting aside all the others as well. They all stand together, because the God of Heaven put them all together.

We do not decide which day of the week is to be kept holy unto God; He alone is to do this. It is for Him to command; it is for us to obey.

Some say that Genesis 2:1-3 is not a command for man to keep the Sabbath, and therefore we do not obey it. But Exodus 16 and 20 clearly show that man *is* commanded to keep it holy. And who dare say that the Ten Commandments were only for the Jewish race? Are the rest of us permitted to lie, steal, cheat, and commit adultery? Are only the Hebrews to observe these ten moral principles?

The reason for the commandment is the Creation of this world: "For in six days the Lord made heaven and earth." This is not something local, merely for a Semitic race;—it is a commandment for all in the entire world who shall bow down and worship their Creator in humble thankfulness for His plan to save them through the life and death of Jesus Christ. It was given at the Creation of this world, and was given to every man, woman, and child who shall live on this planet.

God wrote these Ten Commandments with His own finger (Ex. 31:18; Deut. 9:10). **He wrote them on the most enduring thing in the world,** and that is rock (Ex. 31:18). And He wishes to write them also on our hearts.

"This is the covenant that I will make with them after those days, saith the Lord: I will put My laws into their hearts, and in their minds will I write them."—*Hebrews 10:16 (Heb. 8:10; Jer. 31:33).*

And, if we will let Him, through the New Covenant He will write His holy law upon our hearts. To have the Ten Commandments written on our hearts means two things: First, a willingness to obey them and, second, letting God enable us to do so by the grace of Jesus, His Son. Obedience to God's law is to become an integral part of our lives.

FACT NUMBER FIVE—**The weekly seventh-day Sabbath is part of the Moral Law contained in the Ten Commandments. It will stand forever. The yearly sabbaths were part of the ceremonial laws that prefigured, or foreshadowed, the death and ministry of Christ.**

These "shadow laws," such as Passover and the Wave Sheaf, which were a part of the ceremonial or sacrificial law, would not endure past the death of Christ.

"For the [ceremonial] law having a shadow of good things to come, and not the very image of the things, can never with those sacrifices which they offered year by year continually make the comers thereunto perfect. For then would they not have ceased to be offered? . . But in those sacrifices there is a remembrance again made of sins every year. For it is not possible that the blood of bulls and of goats should take away sins."—*Hebrews 10:1-4.*

These ceremonial laws were not written on rock, but were contained in ordinances, written on parchment. The rock was to endure, but the ordinances that foreshadowed the death of Christ were to pass away at His death. It is for this reason that we do not today observe the yearly sabbaths of the Passover and the Wave Sheaf.

"Blotting out the handwriting of ordinances that was against us, which was contrary to us, and took it out of the way, nailing it to His cross . . Let no man therefore judge you in meat, or in drink, or in respect of an holyday, or of the new moon, or of the sabbath days. Which are a shadow of things to come; but the body is of Christ."—*Colossians 2:14,16-17.*

In the Greek it says, "or of the sabbaths." **There is one weekly Sabbath; it comes down to us from the Creation of this world and will be kept in the New Earth (Isa. 66:22-23). But the yearly sabbaths did not begin until Moses.** They foreshadowed and explained the coming death of Christ till it happened; and, at His death, they were nailed to His cross.

If the ordinances containing the yearly sabbaths had not been set aside at Calvary, we would need now to sacrifice animals on various occasions throughout the year. But we are not now to slay lambs; for Christ, our Passover Lamb, has been sacrificed for us.

"Behold the Lamb of God, which taketh away the sin of the world."—*John 1:29.*

"For even Christ our Passover is sacrificed for us."—*1 Corinthians 5:7.*

FACT NUMBER SIX—Christ's disciples faithfully kept the Bible Sabbath, not Sunday.

The disciples had been with Jesus for three and a half years, and had listened closely to His teachings. What they did at the time of His death on Calvary shows what He taught them. The sacred importance of the seventh-day Sabbath was of such concern to them that they would not even prepare the body of Jesus properly for burial on Friday, lest they transgress the Fourth Commandment.

"And now when the even was come, because it was the preparation, that is, the day before the Sabbath . . Mary Magdalene and Mary the mother of Joses beheld where He was laid.

"And when the Sabbath was past, Mary Magdalene, and Mary the mother of James, and Salome, had bought sweet spices, that they might come and anoint Him. And very early in the morning the first day of the week, they came unto the sepulchre at the rising of the sun. And they said among themselves, Who shall roll us away the stone from the door of the sepulchre?"—*Mark 15:42, 47-16:3.*

For more on this, read Luke 23:53-24:2.

FACT NUMBER SEVEN—According to the New Testament, the Apostles of Jesus always kept the Bible Sabbath.

The Apostles kept the Bible Sabbath (Acts 13:14, 42; 16:13; 17:1-2).

Paul supported himself by tentmaking; and then on the Sabbath, he would preach the gospel.

"Because he was of the same craft, he abode with them, and wrought: for by their occupation, they were tentmakers. And he reasoned in the synagogue every Sabbath, and persuaded the Jews and the Greeks . . He continued there a year and six months, teaching the Word of God among them."—*Acts 18:3-4, 11.*

Paul's manner was the same as Christ's custom: to keep the Bible Sabbath (Acts 17:1-2; Luke 4:16).

Paul never taught that the Moral Law was, or could be, set aside. It will ever govern the conduct of mankind:

"Do we then make void the law through faith? God forbid: yea, we establish the law."—*Romans 3:31.*

"What shall we say then? Shall we continue in sin, that grace may abound? God forbid. How shall we, that are dead to sin, live any longer therein?"—*Romans 6:1-2.*

"What shall we say then? Is the law sin? God forbid. Nay, I had not known sin, but by the law: for I had not known lust, except the law had said, Thou shalt not covet."—*Romans 7:7.*

Paul clearly saw that the problem was that we needed to obey the law; there was nothing wrong with the requirements of the law itself.

"Wherefore the law is holy, and the commandment holy, and just, and good."—*Romans 7:12.*

"Circumcision is nothing, and uncircumcision is nothing, but [that which is important is] the keeping of the commandments of God."—*1 Corinthians 7:19.*

The moral standard that governs mankind was not relaxed or destroyed by the death of Christ; for, indeed, it is through the merits of Christ's sacrifice that we can be empowered to keep that law.

"Thou shalt call His name Jesus, for He shall save His people from their sins."—*Matthew 1:21.*

Jesus saves us from our sins, not in our sins. And since sin is the breaking of the Ten Commandments, it is obvious that He saves us by enabling us, strengthening us, to keep that law.

"Whosoever committeth sin transgresseth also the law: for sin is the transgression of the law."—*1 John 3:4.*

The other Apostles saw this same great truth, that the moral standard that governs mankind, was not relaxed or destroyed by the death of Christ:

"But be ye doers of the Word, and not hearers only, deceiving your own selves. For if any be a hearer of the Word, and not a doer, he is like unto a man beholding his natural face in a glass. For he beholdeth himself, and goeth his way, and straightway forgetteth what manner of man he was.

"But whoso looketh into the perfect law of liberty, and continueth therein, he being not a forgetful hearer, but a doer of the work, this man shall be blessed in his deed . . For whosoever shall keep the whole law, and yet offend in one point, he is guilty of all. For He that saith, Do not commit adultery, said also, Do not kill. Now if thou commit no adultery, yet if thou kill, thou art become a transgressor of the law. So speak ye, and so do, as they that shall be judged by the law of liberty . . Faith, if it hath not works, is dead, being alone. Yea, a man may say, Thou hast faith, and I have works; shew me thy faith without thy works, and I will shew thee my faith by my works."—*James 1:22-25; 2:10-12, 17-18.*

"By this we know that we love the children of God, when we love God, and keep His commandments. For this is the love of God, that we keep His commandments: and His commandments are not grievous."—*1 John 5:2-3.*

FACT NUMBER EIGHT—**God predicted, in Scripture, that men would later try to change the Law of God—and especially the "time law."**

The Bible Sabbath is very important—for it is the very center of our worship of God! If men were later to try to change it to another day, we should surely expect a Bible prophecy saying that it would happen.

"And he [the little horn power] shall speak great words against the most High, and shall wear out the saints of the most High, and think to change times and laws: and they shall be given into His hand until a time and times and the dividing of time."—*Daniel 7:25.*

The church of the Dark Ages was to rule the world for 1260 years, and during this time would try to tear out God's holy Time Law and put a counterfeit in its place. Oh, what blasphemy men can dream up, when they are tempted by Satan to gain religious control of their fellow men!

"For that day [the Second Coming of Christ] shall not come, except there come a falling away first, and that man of sin be revealed, the son of perdition; who opposeth and exalteth himself above all that is called God, or that is worshiped."—*2 Thessalonians 2:3-4.*

God said:

"And hallow My Sabbaths; and they shall be a sign between

Me and you, that ye may know that I am the Lord your God."—
Ezekiel 20:20.

After the New Testament was finished and the Apostles had died, men tried to transfer the sacredness from the seventh to the first day of the week. They tried to change the "time law."

Roman Catholic: "It is well to remind the Presbyterians, Baptists, Methodists, and all other Christians, that the Bible does not support them anywhere in their observance of Sunday. Sunday is an institution of the Roman Catholic Church, and those who observe the day observe a commandment of the Catholic Church."—*Priest Brady, in an address at Elizabeth, N.J., March 17, 1903; reported in the Elizabeth, N.J., News of March 18, 1903.*

"You may search the Bible from Genesis to Revelation, and you will not find a single line authorizing the sanctification of Sunday. The Scriptures enforce the religious observance of Saterday, a day which we never sanctify."—*Cardinal James Gibbon, The Faith of Our Fathers, chapter 8.*

"If Protestants would follow the Bible, they should worship God on the Sabbath day. In keeping the Sunday they are following a law of the Catholic Church."—*Albert Smith, Chancellor of the Archdiocese of Baltimore, replying for the cardinal, in a letter of February 10, 1920.*

"We hold upon this earth the place of God Almighty."—*Pope Leo XIII, Encyclical Letter, June 20, 1894; The Great Encyclical Letters of Leo XIII, p. 304.*

"Prove to me from the Bible alone that I am bound to keep Sunday holy. There is no such law in the Bible. It is a law of the Holy Catholic Church alone. The Bible says 'Remember the Sabbath day to keep it holy.' The Catholic Church says, No. By my divine power I abolish the Sabbath day and command you to keep holy the first day of the week. And lo! The entire civilized world bows down in reverent obedience to the command of the Holy Catholic Church."—*Priest Thomas Enright, CSSR, President of Redemptorist College, Kansas City, MO, in a lecture at Hartford, Kansas Weekly Call, February 22, 1884, and the Ameri-*

can Sentinel, a New York Roman Catholic journal, in June 1893, p. 173.

"Of course the Catholic Church claims that the change was her act . . AND THE ACT IS A MARK of her ecclesiastical power."—*From the office of Cardinal Gibbons, through Chancellor H.F. Thomas, November 11, 1895.*

How important it is that we obey the commandments of God rather than the commandments of men.

"Know ye not, that to whom ye yield yourselves servants to obey, his servants ye are to whom ye obey?"—*Romans 6:16.*

"It is written, Thou shalt worship the Lord thy God, and Him only shalt thou serve."—*Matthew 4:10.*

"But in vain they do worship Me, teaching for doctrines the commandments of men."—*Matthew 15:9.*

"How long halt ye between two opinions? If the Lord be God, follow Him; but if Baal, then follow him."—*1 Kings 18:21.*

FACT NUMBER NINE—**The seventh-day Sabbath, instituted by God at the Creation of this world, is the seal of His governmental authority.**

God's basic governmental code for mankind is the Ten Commandments. Of those ten, only the Sabbath commandment reveals the name of our Creator and Lawgiver.

Of all the commandments in the Decalogue, only the Fourth Commandment reveals the (1) name, (2) authority, and (3) dominion of the Author of this Law:

In six days, (1) the Lord (name) (2) made (office—the Creator) (3) heaven and earth (dominion or territory over which He rules). This commandment alone contains the seal of God.

Examine the notary seal of a notary public or any other legal seal. Each seal will always contain the above three identifying marks.

"Remember the Sabbath day, to keep it holy . . for in six days the Lord made heaven and earth, the sea, and all that in them is, and rested the seventh day: wherefore the Lord blessed the Sabbath day, and hallowed it."—*Exodus 20:8, 11.*

The Sabbath commandment contains the seal of God, and the

Sabbath itself—given in this commandment—is inseparably connected with this seal. For the Sabbath is the basis of all true worship of our Creator. And this worship lies at the heart of all our acknowledgment of His authority as our Creator and our God. The Sabbath is ever to be kept as a sign that we belong to Him. And the keeping of it brings us within the circle of this seal.

The seal is impressed in order that all may know the authority from whence it comes—and that all may know that it is not to be changed. **The seventh-day Sabbath comes from God. Let no man dare to tamper with it**—for the seal of God is upon it.

"Now, O king, establish the decree, and sign the writing, that it be not changed."—*Daniel 6:8.*

"Bind up the testimony, seal the law among My disciples."—*Isaiah 8:16.*

"It [the Sabbath] is a sign between Me and the children of Israel for ever: for in six days the Lord made heaven and earth, and on the seventh day He rested, and was refreshed."—*Exodus 31:17.*

"And hallow My Sabbaths; and they shall be a sign between Me and you, that ye may know that I am the Lord your *God.*"—*Ezekiel 20:20.*

The Sabbath is a powerful sign of God's creative power—not only of this earth, but within our lives as well. It requires the same power to clean our lives and redeem us as it did to create us in the first place.

"Create in me a clean heart, O God."—*Psalm 51:10.*

"We are . . created in Christ Jesus unto good works."—*Ephesians 2:10.*

The Bible tells us there is to be a special sealing work in these last days, just before the return of Jesus in the clouds of heaven.

"And I saw another angel ascending from the east, having the seal of the living God: and he cried with a loud voice to the four angels . . saying, Hurt not the earth, neither the sea, nor the trees, till we have sealed the servants of our God in their foreheads."—*Revelation 7:2-3 (Eze. 9:1-6).*

"And I looked, and, lo, a Lamb stood on the mount Sion, and

with Him an hundred forty and four thousand, having His Father's name written in their foreheads."—*Revelation 14:1.*

The name of the Father is expressive of His character. When Moses asked to see the glory of God, the Lord passed by and told His name—that which He was like:

"The Lord, the Lord God, merciful and gracious, longsuffering, and abundant in goodness and truth."—*Exodus 34:6.*

And as we look at God's holy law, we see another view of His character. It is a transcript of that character. It is God's characteristics written on everlasting stone. He wants us to live it out in our lives.

When God writes His name on your forehead and right hand, this means He writes His law on your heart. This is the work of the new covenant (Heb. 8:10; 10:16; Jer. 31:33); and that work reaches its climax when God "seals in" His own people, just before He returns the second time in the clouds of heaven. What are those sealed ones like? They are fully obedient to the Law of God:

"And in their mouth was found no guile: for they are without fault before the throne of God."—*Revelation 14:5.*

But in the final crisis before His return, there will be a people who will yield obedience to the beast instead of to God.

"And the third angel followed them, saying with a loud voice, If any man worship the beast and his image, and receive his mark in his forehead, or in his hand, the same shall drink of the wine of the wrath of God."—*Revelation 14:9-10.*

"And he [the beast] causeth all, both small and great, rich and poor, free and bond, to receive a mark in their right hand, or in their foreheads."—*Revelation 13:16.*

In contrast with those who serve the beast and receive his mark, are those who in the last days will serve God and receive His seal. How can they be identified? God has told us in His Word. Here is a description of God's remnant people at the end of time:

"And the dragon [Satan, working through his agents] was wroth with the woman [the true church], and went to make war with the remnant of her seed, which keep the commandments of God, and have the testimony of Jesus Christ."—*Revelation 12:17.*

And the third angel of Revelation 14, which warns men to not receive the mark of the beast, also tells them how to avoid receiving it—by keeping the commandments of God through the faith of Jesus Christ:

"And the third angel followed them, saying with a loud voice, If any man worship the beast and his image, and receive his mark in his forehead, or in his hand, the same shall drink of the wine of the wrath of God, which is poured out without mixture . . Here is the patience of the saints: here are they that keep the commandments of God, and the faith of Jesus."—*Revelation 14:9-10, 12.*

The final crisis will be caused by a decree by the beast, that all men must disobey a commandment of the law of God. The nations and churches of the world will not require men to steal or lie or commit adultery. The growing movement toward national Sunday laws is growing stronger every passing year. It is seen that in this point, and in this alone, will be found the heart of the crisis of Revelation 13 and 14.

The first angel of Revelation 14 calls on all men everywhere, today, to reverence God—by returning to the worship of the Creator of all things.

"And I saw another angel fly in the midst of heaven, having the everlasting gospel to preach unto them that dwell on the earth, and to every nation, and kindred, and tongue, and people.

"Saying with a loud voice, Fear God, and give glory to Him; for the hour of His judgment is come: and worship Him that made heaven, and earth, and the sea, and the fountains of waters."—*Revelation 14:6-7.*

As the crisis nears, we must prepare for it.

"The observance of Sunday by the Protestants is an homage they pay, in spite of themselves, to the authority of the [Catholic] Church."—*Monsignor Louis Segur, Plain Talk About the Protestantism of Today, p. 213.*

Already we are facing Sunday closing laws on local levels. Men are prohibited from doing business on the first working day of the week, lest they be fined or imprisoned. And the situation will grow worse in the days just ahead.

"That the image of the beast should both speak, and cause [decree] that as many as would not worship the image of the beast should be killed. And he causeth all, both small and great, rich and poor, free and bond, to receive a mark in their right hand, or in their foreheads: and that no man might buy or sell, save he that had the mark."—*Revelation 13:15-17.*

But there is victory for those who will stand true to the God of heaven. There is overcoming power for those who will "keep the commandments of God and the faith of Jesus" (Rev 14:12).

"And I saw . . them that had gotten the victory over the beast, and over his image, and over his mark, and over the number of his name, stand on the sea of glass, having the harps of God."—*Revelation 15:2.*

FACT NUMBER TEN—**God's remnant people will keep the Bible Sabbath, and that holy day will be kept throughout eternity.**

(1) Even though there are over two thousand denominations today, the remnant people of God, living at the end of time, can be identified. God has identified them for us. After speaking about how the antichrist power in the Dark Ages tried for centuries to destroy the people of God, **we are told how to identify them in these last days, just before Christ returns in the clouds for His own:**

"And the dragon was wroth with the woman, and went to make war with the remnant of her seed, which keep the commandments of God, and have the testimony of Jesus Christ."—*Revelation 12:17.*

And the third angel, after warning all men against receiving the mark of the beast, tells us clearly who will be the little group that will stand apart from this almost universal apostasy:

"Here is the patience of the saints: here are they that keep the commandments of God, and the faith of Jesus."—*Revelation 14:12.*

It will be an almost universal apostasy. All around us can be seen a rising tide of rebellion against the Ten Commandments. The colleges and universities teach that man is but an animal descended from worms and amoeba. The churches teach that God destroyed the

Ten Commandments at Calvary and that Jesus died to take sinners to heaven just as they are. Governmental agencies are relaxing moral restrictions and permitting gambling, abortion, homosexuality, and other vices.

This world is becoming a curse, but soon God will intervene. Prophecy tells us that before the end there will be a small company who will stand true to the commandments of God, by faith in Jesus Christ.

(2) And soon this present evil world will be ended suddenly by the return of Jesus Christ—and heaven will begin for the faithful.

And in that heaven the seventh-day Sabbath will be kept forever. God's people suffered and died for it down here, and they will worship God on that holy day through all ages to come.

Revelation 21 and 22 tells us about this new life with Jesus, when sin has come to an end and the wicked are no longer alive.

"And I saw a new heaven and a new earth: for the first heaven and the first earth were passed away; and there was no more sea . . And he shewed me a pure river of water of life, clear as crystal, proceeding out of the throne of God and of the Lamb."—*Revelation 21:1; 22:1.*

And then **we are told who will enter that beautiful new world:**

"Blessed are they that do His commandments, that they may have right to the tree of life, and may enter in through the gates into the city."—*Revelation 22:14.*

But more: **There is the promise that they will keep the holy Sabbath through all eternity.**

"For, behold, I create new heavens and a new earth: and the former shall not be remembered, nor come into mind . . And they shall build houses, and inhabit them; and they shall plant vineyards, and eat the fruit of them. They shall not build, and another inhabit; they shall not plant, and another eat: for as the days of a tree are the days of My people, and Mine elect shall long enjoy the work of their hands . . The wolf and the lamb shall feed together, and the lion shall eat straw like the bullock; and dust shall be the serpent's meat. They shall not hurt nor destroy in all My holy mountain, saith the Lord . .

"For as the new heavens and the new earth, which I will make, shall remain before Me, saith the Lord, so shall your seed and your name remain. And it shall come to pass, that from one new moon to another, and from one Sabbath to another, shall all flesh come to worship before Me, saith the Lord."—*Isaiah 65:17, 21-22, 25; 66:22-23.*

Now you have seen God's plan for His people. And it is a wonderful one. It can begin for you right now. And it will continue on throughout eternity. Why not begin today—this very week? Ask God to forgive you for the past, and tell Him that, by His grace, you will worship your Creator on His day! This is the best decision you can make. Go to Him just now. He will help you make it.

And next Sabbath—begin that holy walk with God on His day, the holy day of Isaiah 58. Read that chapter and see the blessings He will add, if you will but let Him take over your life.

But think not that there will be no problems or trials. Satan will bring many upon you. He hates the Sabbath and all who will stand loyal to it. Yet if you will determine to be true to God and His Word, you will have strength from above to go through all that lies ahead.

And one day soon, if faithful to the end, you with the redeemed of all ages will rejoice on the sea of glass and will receive from the hand of Jesus the overcomer's crown. And you will be given that new name, expressive of a new character. And you will begin a walk with Jesus that will last through all eternity to come.

"And one of the elders answered, saying unto me, What are these which are arrayed in white robes? and whence come they?

"And I said unto him, Sir, thou knowest. And he said unto me, These are they which came out of great tribulation, and have washed their robes, and made them white in the blood of the Lamb.

"Therefore are they before the throne of God, and serve Him day and night in His temple: and He that sitteth on the throne shall dwell among them.

"They shall hunger no more, neither thirst any more; neither shall the sun light on them, nor any heat.

"For the Lamb which is in the midst of the throne shall feed them, and shall lead them unto living fountains of waters: and God shall wipe away all tears from their eyes."—*Revelation 7:13-17.*

THE BIBLE:
DIVINE GUIDANCE FOR YOUR LIFE

What is the purpose of the Bible?

2 Peter 1:21—"For the prophecy came not in old time by the will of man, but holy men of God spake as they were moved by the Holy Ghost."

John 20:30-31—"And many other signs truly did Jesus in the presence of His disciples, which are not written in this book: But these are written, that ye might believe that Jesus is the Christ, the Son of God; and that believing ye might have life through His name."

Psalm 119:11—"Thy Word have I hid in mine heart, that I might not sin against Thee."

Psalm 119:105—"Thy Word is a lamp unto my feet, and a light unto my path."

Romans 15:4—"For whatsoever things were written aforetime were written for our learning, that we through patience and comfort of the Scriptures might have hope."

How should we study the Bible?

Acts 17:11—"These were more noble than those in Thessalonica, in that they received the Word with all readiness of mind, and searched the Scriptures daily, whether those things were so."

Isaiah 28:10—"For precept must be upon precept, precept upon precept; line upon line, line upon line; here a little, and there a little."

2 Timothy 2:15—"Study to show thyself approved unto God, a workman that needeth not to be ashamed, rightly dividing the word of truth."

John 5:39—"Search the Scriptures, for in them ye think ye have eternal life; and they are they which testify of Me."

THE PLAN OF REDEMPTION:
GOD'S PLAN TO SAVE YOU FROM SIN

Romans 3:23—"For all have sinned and come short of the glory of God."

Isaiah 59:2—"But your iniquities have separated between you and your God, and your sins have hid His face from you, that He will not hear."

Romans 6:23—"For the wages of sin is death; but the gift of God is eternal life through Jesus Christ our Lord."

2 Peter 3:9—"The Lord is not slack concerning His promise, as some men count slackness; but is longsuffering to us-ward, not willing that any should perish, but that all should come to repentance."

Exodus 34:6-7—"The Lord God, merciful and gracious, long-suffering, and abundant in goodness and truth, keeping mercy for thousands, forgiving iniquity and transgression and sin, and that will by no means clear the guilty."

John 3:16-20—"For God so loved the world, that He gave His only begotten Son, that whosoever believeth in Him should not perish, but have everlasting life. For God sent not His Son into the world to condemn the world; but that the world through Him might be saved. He that believeth on Him is not condemned: but he that believeth not is condemned already, because he hath not believed in the name of the only begotten Son of God. And this is the condemnation, that light is come into the world, and men loved darkness rather than light, because their deeds were evil. For every one that doeth evil hateth the light, neither cometh to the light, lest his deeds should be reproved."

Luke 19:10—"For the Son of man is come to seek and to save that which was lost."

Matthew 1:21—"He shall save His people from their sins."

Isaiah 53:6—"All we like sheep have gone astray; we have turned every one to his own way; and the Lord hath laid on him the iniquity of us all."

Acts 16:31—"Believe on the Lord Jesus Christ, and thou shalt be saved."

2 Corinthians 6:2—"Now is the accepted time; behold, now is the day of salvation."

John 1:12—"But as many as received Him, to them gave He power to become the sons of God, even to them that believe on His name."

Galatians 2:20—"I am crucified with Christ: nevertheless I live; yet not I, but Christ liveth in me: and the life which I now live in the flesh I live by the faith of the Son of God, who loved me, and gave Himself for me."

John 3:3—"Verily, verily, I say unto thee, Except a man be born again, he cannot see the kingdom of God."

2 Corinthians 5:17—"Therefore if any man be in Christ, he is a new creature: old things are passed away; behold, all things are become new."

Philippians 2:13—"For it is God which worketh in you both to will and to do of His good pleasure."

Hebrews 10:16—"I will put My laws into their hearts, and in their minds will I write them."

1 John 1:9—"If we confess our sins, He is faithful and just to forgive us our sins, and to cleanse us from all unrighteousness."

Philippians 4:13—"I can do all things through Christ which strengtheneth me."

OBEDIENCE BY FAITH:
HOW GOD ENABLES YOU TO OBEY HIM

1 - GOD HAS A GOVERNMENT

Psalm 103:19—"The Lord hath prepared His throne in the heavens; and His kingdom ruleth over all."

2 - THERE CAN BE NO GOVERNMENT WITHOUT LAW

Romans 7:12—"The law is holy, and the commandment holy, and just, and good."

Romans 7:14—"For we know that the law is spiritual: but I am carnal, sold under sin."

Proverbs 28:9—"He that turneth away his ear from hearing the law, even his prayer shall be abomination."

3 - GOD'S LAW WAS FOR MEN IN BIBLE TIMES

Romans 3:31—"Do we then make void the law through faith? God forbid: yea, we establish the law."

James 2:10-12—"For whosoever shall keep the whole law, and yet offend in one point, he is guilty of all. For He that said, Do not commit adultery, said also Do not kill. Now if thou commit no adultery yet if thou kill, thou art become a transgressor of the law. So speak ye, and so do, as they that shall be judged by the law of liberty."

4 - GOD'S LAW IS FOR THE REMNANT IN THE LAST DAYS

Revelation 12:17—"And the dragon was wroth with the woman, and went to make war with the remnant of her seed, which keep the commandments of God, and have the testimony of Jesus Christ."

Revelation 14:12—"Here is the patience of the saints: here are they that keep the commandments of God, and the faith of Jesus" *(also verses 13-15).*

5 - THERE IS GENERAL REBELLION AGAINST GOD'S LAW

Romans 8:7—"The carnal mind is enmity against God: for it is not subject to the law of God, neither indeed can be."

Psalm 119:126—"It is time for Thee, Lord, to work: for they have made void Thy law."

6 - THERE ARE PROMISES FOR THE OBEDIENT

Psalm 119:165—"Great peace have they which love Thy law: and nothing shall offend them."

Isaiah 48:18—"O that thou hadst hearkened to My commandments! then had thy peace been as a river, and thy righteousness as the waves of the sea."

7 - THE SACRIFICIAL LAWS WERE ABOLISHED AT THE CROSS (Hebrews 10:1-16)

Colossians 2:14—"Blotting out the handwriting of ordinances that was against us, which was contrary to us, and took it out of the way, nailing it to His cross."

Colossians 2:17—"Which are a shadow of things to come; but the body is of Christ."

8 - WHAT DOES THE LAW DO FOR THE SINNER?

God uses the law to do for the sinner just what needs to be done. The sinner must realize that he is a sinner. The heavy hand of the law must be laid upon him, and he must be arrested in his course. Notice the following carefully:

1. It gives a knowledge of sin.

Romans 3:20—"By the law is the knowledge of sin" (Rom. 7:7).

2. It brings guilt and condemnation.

Romans 3:19—"Now we know that what things soever the law saith, it saith to them who are under the law: that every mouth may be stopped, and all the world may become guilty before God."

3. It acts as a spiritual mirror.

James 1:23-25—"If any be a hearer of the Word, and not a doer, he is like unto a man beholding his natural face in a glass: for he beholdeth himself, and goeth his way, and straightway forgetteth what manner of man he was. But whoso looketh into the perfect law of liberty, and continueth therein, he being not a forgetful hearer, but a doer of the work, this man shall be blessed in his deed" *(aso James 2:9-12)*.

Without the law, the sinner is like a man who is afflicted with a deadly disease that he doesn't know he has. Paul said, "I had not known sin, but by the law" (Rom. 7:7).

9 - WHAT IS THE LAW UNABLE TO DO FOR THE SINNER?

The law cannot forgive. Law does not possess the power to forgive those who transgress its precepts. Only the Lawgiver can do that. Jesus died to redeem us from the curse of the law (Gal. 3:13). The law cannot keep the sinner from sinning because "the carnal mind is enmity against God: for it is not subject to the law of God, neither indeed can be" (Rom. 8:7).

The law only shows the sinner where he needs to change; but the law, itself, cannot change him. And so let us get three facts about the law very clear.

1. It cannot forgive or justify.

Romans 3:20—"By the deeds of the law there shall no flesh be justified in His sight."

2. It cannot keep from sin or sanctify.

Galatians 3:21—"Is the law then against the promises of God? God forbid: for if there had been a law given which could have given life, verily righteousness should have been by the law."

3. It cannot cleanse or keep the heart clean (Rom. 9:3, 7-8).

The law is limited in its ability to do all that needs to be done for the sinner. A wound cannot be sewed up with only a needle. The thread of the gospel must do that.

10 - WHAT DOES THE GRACE OF CHRIST DO FOR THE SINNER?

When the law of God and the Spirit of God have made the sinner conscious of his sin, he will then feel his need of Christ and go to the Saviour for pardon. The publican found it so (Luke 18:13-14). The woman taken in adultery felt condemned and ashamed. She needed sympathy and forgiveness, and Christ was ready to grant these to her. Then He said, "Sin no more."

If we confess and put away sin, He will forgive (1 John 1:9). This is grace, or unmerited favor. This gracious love of Christ awakens love in the heart of the sinner, and he then desires to serve and obey God. Here are four elements of the saving grace of Christ:

1. It forgives and justifies.

Acts 13:38-39—"Be it known unto you therefore, men and brethren, that through this man is preached unto you the forgiveness of sins: and by Him all that believe are justified from all things, from which ye could not be justified by the law of Moses" (Luke 18:13-14).

2. It saves from sin, or sanctifies.

Matthew 1:21—"She shall bring forth a son, and thou shalt call His name Jesus: for He shall save His people from their sins."

1 Corinthians 1:30—"But of Him are ye in Christ Jesus, who of God is made unto us wisdom, and righteousness, and sanctification, and redemption."

3. It inspires faith.

Ephesians 2:8-10—"By grace are ye saved through faith; and that not of yourselves: it is the gift of God: not of works, lest any man should boast. For we are His workmanship, created in Christ Jesus unto good works, which God hath before ordained that we should walk in them."

4. It brings God's power.

Romans 1:16—"I am not ashamed of the gospel of Christ: for it is the power of God unto salvation to every one that believeth; to the

Jew first, and also to the Greek."

Forgiveness of sin and power over sin come through the exercise of simple faith in God's promises and a full surrender of the heart to Him.

11 - HOW DOES A SINNER SAVED BY GRACE RELATE TO THE LAW?

1. The law becomes the standard of his life.

1 John 5:3—"This is the love of God, that we keep His commandments."

2. He permits Christ to fulfill in him the righteousness of the law.

Romans 8:3-4—"God sending His own Son in the likeness of sinful flesh, and for sin, condemned sin in the flesh: that the righteousness of the law might be fulfilled in us, who walk not after the flesh, but after the Spirit."

3. Christ writes the law in his heart.

Hebrews 8:10—"This is the covenant that I will make with the house of Israel after those days, saith the Lord; I will put My laws into their mind, and write them in their hearts: and I will be to them a God, and they shall be to Me a people" (also Ps. 119:11).

"Thou wilt keep him in perfect peace,
whose mind is stayed on Thee; because
He trusteth in Thee. Trust ye in the Lord for
ever; for in the Lord Jehovah is everlasting
strength."

—Isaiah 26:3-4

"The Lord is nigh unto them that are of a
broken heart, and saveth such as be of a
contrite spirit."

—Psalm 34:18

Chapter Seven

Entering upon a New Way of Life

— The Basic Steps to Christ

It is not money, power, or human affection that you crave. Your greatest need is acceptance by God.

How can you have it? How can you find Him? How can you be accepted by Him? How can you stay close to Him?

There are answers, and they are not complicated.

Here is what you have always wanted: peace with God! —

– Part One –
How Can I Come to God?

Nature and revelation alike testify of God's love. It is transgression of God's law—the law of love—that has brought woe and death. Yet even amid the suffering that results from sin, God's love is revealed. "God is love" is written upon every opening bud, upon every spire of springing grass.

Jesus came to live among men to reveal the infinite love of God. Love, mercy, and compassion were revealed in every act of His life; His heart went out in tender sympathy to the children of men. He took man's nature, that He might reach man's wants. The poorest and humblest were not afraid to approach Him. Such is the character of Christ as revealed in His life. This is the character of God.

Summary of all the key points in the book,
Steps to Christ, in the author's own words.

It was to redeem us that Jesus lived and suffered and died. He became a "Man of Sorrows," that we might be made partakers of everlasting joy. But this great sacrifice was not made in order to create in the Father's heart a love for man, not make Him willing to save. No, no! "God so loved the world, that He gave His only-begotten Son." *John 3:16*. The Father loves us, not because of the great propitiation, but He provided the propitiation because He loves us. None but the Son of God could accomplish our redemption.

What a value this places upon man! Through transgression the sons of man become subjects of Satan. Through faith in the atoning sacrifice of Christ the sons of Adam may become the sons of God. The matchless love of God for a world that did not love Him! The thought has a subduing power upon the soul and brings the mind into captivity to the will of God.

Man was originally endowed with noble powers and a well-balanced mind. He was perfect in his being, and in harmony with God. His thoughts were pure, his aims holy. But through disobedience, his powers were perverted, and selfishness took the place of love. His nature became so weakened through transgression that it was impossible for him, in his own strength, to resist the power of evil.

It is impossible for us, of ourselves, to escape from the pit of sin in which we are sunken. Our hearts are evil, and we cannot change them. There must be a power working from within, a new life from above, before men can be changed from sin to holiness. That power is Christ. His grace alone can quicken the lifeless faculties of the soul, and attract it to God, to holiness. To all, there is but one answer, "Behold the Lamb of God, which taketh away the sin of the world" (John 1:29). Let us avail ourselves of the means provided for us that we may be transformed into His likeness, and be restored to fellowship with the ministering angels, to harmony and communion with the Father and the Son.

How shall a man be just with God? How shall the sinner be made righteous? It is only through Christ that we can be brought into harmony with God, with holiness; but how are we to come to Christ?

Repentance includes sorrow for sin and a turning away from it. We shall not renounce sin unless we see its sinfulness; until we turn away from it in heart, there will be no real change in the life.

But when the heart yields to the influence of the Spirit of God, the conscience will be quickened, and the sinner will discern something of the depth and sacredness of God's holy law, the foundation of His government in heaven and on earth. Conviction takes hold upon the mind and heart.

The prayer of David, after his fall, illustrates the nature of true sorrow for sin. His repentance was sincere and deep. There was no effort to palliate his guilt; no desire to escape the judgment threatened, inspired his prayer David saw the enormity of his transgression; he saw the defilement of his soul; he loathed his sin. It was not for pardon only that he prayed, but for purity of heart. He longed for the joy of holiness, to be restored to harmony and communion with God. A repentance such as this, is beyond the reach of our own power to accomplish; it is obtained only from Christ.

Christ is ready to set us free from sin, but He does no force the will. If we refuse, what more can He do? Study God's Word prayerfully. As you see the enormity of sin, a you see yourself as you really are, do not give up in despair. It was sinners that Christ came to save. When Satan comes to tell you that you are a great sinner, look to you Redeemer and talk of His merits. Acknowledge your sin but tell the enemy that "Christ came into the world to save sinners" and that you may be saved (1 Tim. 1:15).

"He that covereth his sins shall not prosper: but whoso confesseth and forsaketh them shall have mercy." *Proverbs 28:13*. The conditions of obtaining mercy of God are simple and just and reasonable. Confess your sins to God who only can forgive them, and your faults to one another Those who have not humbled their souls before God is acknowledging their guilt, have not yet fulfilled the first step of acceptance. We must be willing to humble our hearts and comply with the conditions of the Word of truth. The confession that is the outpouring of the inmost soul finds its way to the God of infinite pity. True confession is always of a specific character, and acknowledges particular sins. All confession should be definite and to the point. It is written, "If we confess our sins, He is faithful and just to forgive us our sins, and to cleanse us from all unrighteousness" (1 John 1:9).

God's promise is, "Ye shall seek Me, and find Me, when ye shall search for Me with all your heart." *Jeremiah 29:13.* The whole heart must be yielded, or the change can never be wrought in us by which we are to be restored to His likeness.

The warfare against self is the greatest battle that was ever fought. The yielding of self, surrendering all to the will of God, requires a struggle; but the soul must submit to God before it can be renewed in holiness.

In giving ourselves to God, we must necessarily give up all that would separate us from Him. There are those who profess to serve God, while they rely upon their own efforts to obey His law, to form a right character, and secure slavation. Their hearts are not moved by any deep sense of the love of Christ, but they seek to perform the duties of the Christian life as that which God requires of them in order to gain heaven. Such religion is worthless.

When Christ dwells in the heart, the soul will be so filled with His love, with the joy of communion with Him, that it will cleave to Him; and in the contemplation of Him, self will be forgotten. Love to Christ will be the spring of action. Such do not ask for the lowest standard, but aim at perfect conformity to the will of their Redeemer.

Do you feel that it is too great a sacrifice to yield all to Christ? Ask yourself the question, "What has Christ given for me?" The Son of God gave all—life and love and suffering—for our redemption. And can it be that we, the unworthy objects of so great love, will withhold our hearts from Him? What do we give up, when we give all? A sin-polluted heart, for Jesus to purify, to cleanse by His own blood, and to save by His matchless love. And yet men think it hard to give up all! God does not require us to give up anything that it is for our best interest to retain. In all that He does, He has the well-being of His children in view.

Many are inquiring, "*How* am I to make the surrender of myself to God?" You desire to give yourself to Him, but you are weak in moral power, in slavery to doubt, and controlled by the habits of your life of sin. Your promises and resolutions are like ropes of sand. You cannot control your thoughts, your impulses, your affections. The knowledge of your broken promises and forfeited pledges weakens your confidence in your own sincerity, and causes you to feel that God cannot accept you; but you need not despair.

What you need to understand is the true force of the will. This is the governing power in the nature of man, the power of decision, or of choice. Everything depends on the right action of the will. The power of choice God has given to men; it is theirs to exercise. You cannot change your heart, you cannot of yourself give to God its affections; but you can *choose* to serve Him. You can give Him your will; He will then work in you to will and to do according to His good pleasure. Thus your whole nature will be brought under the control of the Spirit of Christ; your affections will be centered upon Him, your thoughts will be in harmony with Him.

Desires for goodness and holiness are right as far as they go; but if you stop here, they will avail nothing. Many will be lost while hoping and desiring to be Christians. They do not come to the point of yielding the will to God. They do not *now choose* to be Christians.

Through the right exercise of the will, an entire change may be made in your life. You will have strength from above to hold you steadfast, and thus through constant surrender to God you will be enabled to live the new life, even the life of faith.

As your conscience has been quickened by the Holy

pirit, you have seen something of the evil of sin, of its
ower, its guilt, its woe; and you look upon it with abhor-
ence. It is peace that you need. You have confessed your
ns, and in heart put them away. You have resolved to give
ourself to God. Now go to Him, and ask that He will wash
way your sins and give you a new heart.

Then believe that He does this *because He has prom-
ed.* The gift which God promises us, we must believe we
o receive, and it is ours. You are a sinner. You cannot
tone for your past sins; you cannot change your heart and
ake yourself holy. But God promises to do all this for you
rough Christ. You *believe* that promise. You confess your
ns and give yourself to God. You will to serve Him. Just
s surely as you do this, God will fulfill His Word to you. If
ou believe the promise,—God supplies the fact. Do not
ait to *feel* that you are made whole, but say, "I believe it;
is so, not because I feel it, but because God promised."

*—Summary of all the key points in Steps to Christ, pp. 9-51,
in the author's own words.*

– Part Two –
How Can I Remain True to God?

Jesus says, "What things soever ye desire, when ye
ray, believe that ye receive them, and ye shall have them"
Mark 11:24). There is a condition to this promise—that
e pray according to the will of God. But it is the will of
od to cleanse us from sin, to make us His children, and to
able us to live a holy life. So we may ask for these bless-
gs, and believe that we receive them, and thank God that
e *have* received them.

Henceforth you are not your own; you are bought with
price. Through this simple act of believing God, the Holy
pirit has begotten a new life in your heart. You are a child
orn into the family of God, and He loves you as He loves
is Son.

Now that you have given yourself to Jesus, do not draw back, do not take yourself away from Him, but day by day say, "I am Christ's; I have given myself to Him"; and ask Him to give you His Spirit and keep you by His grace. As it is by giving yourself to God, and believing Him, that you become His child, so you are to live in Him.

Here is where thousands fail; they do not believe that Jesus pardons them personally, individually. They do not take God at His Word. It is the privilege of all who comply with the conditions to know for themselves that pardon is freely extended for every sin. Put away the suspicion that God's promises are not meant for you. They are for every repentant transgressor.

Look up, you that are doubting and trembling; for Jesus lives to make intercession for us. Thank God for the gift of His dear Son.

"If any man be in Christ, he is a new creature: old things are passed away; behold, all things are become new." *2 Corinthians 5:17.*

A person may not be able to tell the exact time or place, or trace all the chain of circumstances in the process of conversion; but this does not prove him to be unconverted. A change will be seen in the character, the habits, the pursuits. The contrast will be clear and decided between what they have been and what they have become. Who has the heart? With whom are our thoughts? Of whom do we love to converse? Who has our warmest affections and our best energies? If we are Christ's, our thoughts are with Him. There is no evidence of genuine repentance unless it works reformation. The loveliness of the character of Christ will be seen in His followers. It was His delight to do the will of God.

There are two errors against which the children of God especially need to guard: The first is that of looking to their own works, trusting to anything they can do, to bring themselves into harmony with God. All that man can do without Christ is polluted with selfishness and sin. It is the grace of Christ alone, through faith, which can make us holy.

The opposite and no less dangerous error is that belief in Christ releases men from keeping the law of God; that since by faith alone we become partakers of the grace of Christ, our works have nothing to do with our redemption.

Obedience is the fruit of faith. Righteousness is defined by the standard of God's holy law, as expressed in the ten commandments (Exo. 20:3-20). That so-called faith in Christ, which professes to release men from the obligation of obedience to God, is not faith, but presumption. The condition of eternal life is now just what it always has been,—just what it was in paradise before the fall of our first parents,—perfect obedience to the law of God, perfect righteousness. If eternal life were granted on any condition short of this, then the happiness of the whole universe would be imperiled. The way would be open for sin, with all its train of woe and misery, to be immortalized.

Christ changes the heart. He abides in your heart by faith. You are to maintain this connection with Christ by faith and the continual surrender of your will to Him; and so long as you do this, He will work in you to will and to do according to His good pleasure.

The closer you come to Jesus, the more faulty you will appear in your own eyes; for your vision will be clearer. This is evidence that Satan's delusions are losing their power. No deep-seated love for Jesus can dwell in the heart that does not realize its own sinfulness. The soul that is transformed by the grace of Christ will admire His character. A view of our sinfulness drives us to Him who can pardon; and when the soul, realizing its helplessness, reaches out after Christ, He will reveal Himself in power. The more our sense of need drives us to Him and to the Word of God, the more exalted views we shall have of His character, and the more fully we shall reflect His image.

The change of heart by which we become children of God is in the Bible spoken of as birth. Again it is compared to the germination of the good seed sown by the husbandman. It is God who brings the bud to bloom and the flower to fruit. It is by His power that the seed develops.

As the flower turns to the sun, that the bright beams may aid in perfecting its beauty and symmetry, so should we turn to the Sun of Righteousness, that heaven's light may shine upon us, that our character may be developed into the likeness of Christ.

Do you ask, "How am I to abide in Christ?" In the same way as you received Him at first. "As ye have therefore received Christ Jesus the Lord, so walk in Him." *Colossians 2:6.* By faith you became Christ's, and by faith you are to grow up in Him—by giving and taking. You are to give all,—your heart, your will, your service,—give yourself to Him to obey all His requirements; and you must take all—Christ, the fullness of all blessing, to abide in your heart, to be your strength, your righteousness, your everlasting helper—to give you power to obey.

Consecrate yourself to God in the morning; make this your very first work. Let your prayer be, "Take me, O Lord, as wholly Thine. I lay all my plans at Thy feet. Use me today in Thy service. Abide with me, and let all my work be wrought in Thee." This is a daily matter. Each morning consecrate yourself to God for that day. Surrender all your plans to Him, to be carried out or given up as His providence shall indicate. Thus day by day you may be giving your life into the hands of God, and thus your life will be molded more and more after the life of Christ.

A life in Christ is a life of restfulness. There may be no ecstasy of feeling, but there should be an abiding, peaceful trust. When the mind dwells upon self, it is turned away from Christ, the source of strength and life. Hence, it is Satan's constant effort to keep the attention diverted from the Saviour and thus prevent the union and communion of the soul with Christ.

When Christ took human nature upon Him, He bound humanity to Himself by a tie of love that can never be broken by any power save the choice of man himself. Satan will constantly present allurements to induce us to break this tie—to choose to separate ourselves from Christ. But let us keep our eyes fixed upon Christ, and He will preserve us. Looking unto Jesus, we are safe. Nothing can pluck us out of His hand. All that Christ was to the disciples, He desires to be to His children today.

Jesus prayed for us, and He asked that we might be one with Him, even as He is one with the Father. What a union is this! Thus, loving Him and abiding in Him, we shall "grow up into Him in all things, which is the head, even Christ" (Ephesians 4:15).

God is the source of life and light and joy to the universe. Wherever the life of God is in the hearts of men, it will flow out to others in love and blessing.

Our Saviour's joy was in the uplifting and redemption of fallen men. For this He counted not His life dear to Himself, but endured the cross, despising the shame. When the love of Christ is enshrined in the heart, like sweet fragrance it cannot be hidden. Love to Jesus will be manifested in a desire to work as He worked for the blessing and uplifting of humanity. It will lead to love, tenderness, and sympathy toward all the creatures of our heavenly Father's care. Those who are the partakers of the grace of Christ will be ready to make any sacrifice, that others for whom He died may share the heavenly gift. They will do all they can to make the world better for their stay in it. This spirit is the sure outgrowth of a soul truly converted. No sooner does one come to Christ than there is born in his heart a desire to make known to others what a precious friend he has found in Jesus. If we have tasted and seen that the Lord is good, we shall have something to tell. We shall seek to present to others the attractions of Christ and the unseen realities of the world to come. There will be an intensity of desire to follow in the path that Jesus trod.

And the effort to bless others will react in blessings upon ourselves. Those who thus become participants in labors of love are brought nearest to their Creator. The spirit of unselfish labor for others gives depth, stability, and Christlike loveliness to the character, and brings peace and happiness to its possessor. Strength comes by exercise. We need not go to heathen lands, or even leave the narrow circle of the home, if it is there that our duty lies, in order to work for Christ. With a loving spirit we may perform life's humblest duties "unto the Lord" (Col. 3:23). If the love of God is in the heart, it will be manifested in the life. You are not to wait for great occasions or to expect extraordinary abilities before you go to work for God. The humblest and poorest of the disciples of Jesus can be a blessing to others.

Many are the ways in which God is seeking to make Himself known to us and bring us into communion with Him. If we will but listen, Nature speaks to our senses without ceasing. God's created works will teach us precious lessons of obedience and trust.

No tears are shed that God does not notice. There is no smile that He does not mark. If we would but fully believe this, all undue anxieties would be dismissed. Our lives would not be so filled with disappointment as now; for everything, whether great or small, would be left in the hands of God.

God speaks to us through His providential works and through the influence of His Spirit upon the heart. God speaks to us in His Word. Here we have in clearer lines the revelation of His character, of His dealings with men, and the great work of redemption. Fill the whole heart with the words of God. They are the living water, quenching your burning thirst. They are the living bread from heaven.

The theme of redemption is one that the angels desire to look into; it will be the science and the song of the redeemed throughout the ceaseless ages of eternity. Is it not worthy of careful thought and study now? As we meditate upon the Saviour, there will be a hungering and thirsting of soul to become like Him whom we adore.

The Bible was written for the common people. The great truths necessary for salvation are made as clear as noonday. There is nothing more calculated to strengthen the intellect than the study of the Scriptures. But there is little benefit derived from a hasty reading of the Bible. One passage studied, until its significance is clear to the mind and its relation to the plan of salvation is evident, is of more value than the perusal of many chapters with no definite purpose in view and no positive instruction gained.

Keep your Bible with you. As you have opportunity, read it; fix the texts in your memory.

We cannot obtain wisdom without earnest attention and prayerful study. Never should the Bible be studied without prayer. Before opening its pages, we should ask for the enlightenment of the Holy Spirit, and it will be given. Angels from the world of light will be with those who in humility of heart seek for divine guidance. How must God esteem the human race, since He gave His Son to die for them and appoints His Holy Spirit to be man's teacher and continual guide!

Through nature and revelation, through His providence, and by the influence of His Spirit, God speaks to us. But these are not enough; we need also to pour out our hearts to Him. In order to commune with God, we must have something to say to Him concerning our actual life.

Prayer is the opening of the heart to God as to a friend. Not that it is necessary in order to make known to God what we are, but in order to enable us to receive Him. Prayer does not bring God down to us, but brings us up to Him.

Our heavenly Father waits to bestow upon us the fullness of His blessing. What a wonder it is that we pray so little! God is ready and willing to hear the sincere prayer of the humblest of His children. What can the angels of heaven think of poor helpless human beings, who are subject to temptation, when God's heart of infinite love yearns toward them, ready to give them more than they can ask or think, and yet they pray so little and have so little faith?

The darkness of the evil one encloses those who neglect to pray. The whispered temptations of the enemy entice them to sin; and it is all because they do not make use of prayer. Yet prayer is the key in the hand of faith to unlock heaven's storehouse, where are treasured the boundless resources of Omnipotence.

There are certain conditions upon which we may expect that God will hear and answer our prayers:

One is that we feel our need of help from Him. If we regard iniquity in our hearts, if we cling to any known sin, the Lord will not hear us; but the prayer of the penitent, contrite soul is always accepted. When all known wrongs are righted, we may believe that God will answer our petitions.

Another element of prevailing prayer is faith. When our prayers seem not to be answered, we are to cling to the promise; for the time of answering will surely come, and we shall receive the blessing we need most. But to claim that prayer will always be answered in the very way and for the particular thing that we desire, is presumption.

When we come to God in prayer, we should have a spirit of love and forgiveness in our own hearts.

Perseverance in prayer has been made a condition of receiving. We must pray always if we would grow in faith and experience.

We should pray in the family circle, and above all we must not neglect secret prayer, for this is the life of the soul. Family or public prayer alone is not sufficient. Secret prayer is to be heard only by the prayer-hearing God.

There is no time or place in which it is inappropriate to offer up a petition to God. In the crowds of the street, in the midst of a business engagement, we may send up a petition to God and plead for divine guidance.

Let the soul be drawn out and upward, that God may grant us a breath of the heavenly atmosphere. We may keep so near to God that in every unexpected trial our thoughts will turn to Him as naturally as the flower turns to the sun. Keep your wants, your joys, your sorrows, your cares, and your fears before God. You cannot burden Him; you cannot weary Him. He is not indifferent to the wants of His children.

We sustain a loss when we neglect the privilege of associating together to strengthen and encourage one another in the service of God. If Christians would associate together, speaking to each other of the love of God and the precious truths of redemption, their own hearts would be refreshed and they would refresh one another.

·We must gather about the cross. Christ and Him crucified should be the theme of contemplation, of conversation, and of our most joyful emotion. We should keep in our thoughts every blessing we receive from God, and when we realize His great love we should be willing to trust everything to the hand that was nailed to the cross for us.

The soul may ascend nearer heaven on the wings of praise. As we express our gratitude, we are approximating to the worship of the heavenly hosts.

Many are at times troubled with the suggestions of skepticism. God never asks us to believe, without giving sufficient evidence upon which to base our faith. Disguise it as they may, the real cause of doubt and skepticism, in most cases, is the love of sin. We must have a sincere desire to know the truth and a willingness of heart to obey it.

—Summary of Steps to Christ, pages 51 to 111, in the author's own words.

Chapter 7 is condensed, in the author's own words, from the book, *Steps to Christ.*

Chapters 1 through 5 are condensed, in the author's own words, from the 88 edition of the extremely important book, *Great Controversy,* as follows:

CHAPTER 1 includes all of *Great Controversy, chapter 29.*

CHAPTER 2 focuses on *Great Controversy, chapters 1, 2 and 3,* but also includes portions of *chapters 8, 16, and 26.*

CHAPTER 3 covers the greater part of *Great Controversy, chapter 25,* and much of *chapter 35.*

CHAPTER 4 has a large amount of material from the very important *chapters 33 and 34.*

CHAPTER 5 brings together the best of *chapters 27, 35, 36, 37, 38, 40, and 42.*

Chapter Eight

Principles of Healthful Living
— Another Preparation for the Crisis

We do not have to be sick all the time. **The laws of nature are the laws of God. Learning them and obeying them can enable each of us to live a fuller, happier life.** Our minds will be clearer, our bodies stronger, and we will be able to better serve our God.

Here are principles of healthful living which can help you —

We today are so accustomed to chemical drug medications, that it is surprising to learn that the natural healing centers of a hundred years ago used a combination of eight natural principles (pure air, sunlight, abstemiousness, rest, exercise, proper diet, the use of water, and trust in divine power) to restore health from nearly every type of disease—without the dangerous side effects of drugs, all of which are poisonous to one extent or another. Here are helpful statements from that earlier era, written by the author of chapters 1-5 and 7:

"A practice that is laying the foundation of a vast amount of disease and of even more serious evils, is the free use of poisonous drugs. When attacked by disease, many will not take the trouble to search out the cause of their illness. Their chief anxiety is to rid themselves of pain and inconvenience. So they resort to patent nostrums, of whose real properties they know little, or they apply to a physician for some remedy to counteract the result of their misdoing; but with no thought of making a change in their unhealthful habits. If immediate benefit is not realized, another medicine is tried, and then another. Thus the evil continues.

"People need to be taught that drugs do not cure disease. It is true that they sometimes afford present relief, and the patient appears to recover as the result of their use; this is because nature has sufficient vital force to expel the poison and to correct the conditions that caused the disease. Health is recovered in spite of the drug. But in most cases the drug only changes the form and location of the disease. Often the effect of the poison seems to be overcome for a time, but the results remain in the system, and work great harm at some later period.

"By the use of poisonous drugs, many bring upon themselves lifelong illness, and many lives are lost that might be saved by the use of natural methods of healing. The poisons contained in many so-called remedies create habits and appetites that mean ruin to both soul and body . .

"The only hope of better things is in the education of the people in right principles. Let physicians teach the people that restorative power is not in drugs, but in nature. Disease is an effort of nature to free the system from conditions that result from a violation of the laws of health. In case of sickness, the cause should be ascertained. Unhealthful conditions should be changed, wrong habits corrected. Then nature is to be assisted in her effort to expel impurities and to reestablish right conditions in the system.

"**Pure air, sunlight, abstemiousness, rest, exercise, proper diet, the use of water, trust in divine power,**—these are the true remedies. Every person should have a knowledge of nature's remedial agencies and how to apply them. It is essential both to understand the principles involved in the treatment of the sick and to have a practical training that will enable one rightly to use this knowledge.

"The use of natural remedies requires an amount of care and effort that many are not willing to give. Nature's process of healing and upbuilding is gradual, and to the impatient it seems slow. The surrender of hurtful indulgences requires sacrifice.

But in the end it will be found that nature, untrammeled, does her work wisely and well. Those who persevere in obedience to her laws will reap the reward in health of body and health of mind . .

"We cannot be too often reminded that health does not depend on chance. It is a result of obedience to law . . It is not mimic battles in which we are engaged. We are waging a warfare upon which hang eternal results. We have unseen enemies to meet. Evil angels are striving for the dominion of every human being. Whatever injures the health, not only lessens physical vigor, but tends to weaken the mental and moral powers. Indulgence in any unhealthful practice makes it more difficult for one to discriminate between right and wrong, and hence more difficult to resist evil. It increases the danger of failure and defeat . .

"Apart from divine power; no genuine reform can be effected. Human barriers against natural and cultivated tendencies are but as the sandbank against the torrent. Not until the life of Christ becomes a vitalizing power in our lives can we resist the temptations that assail us from within and from without.

"Christ came to this world and lived the law of God, that man might have perfect mastery over the natural inclinations which corrupt the soul. The Physician of soul and body, He gives victory over warring lusts. He has provided every facility, that man may possess completeness of character."—*Ministry of Healing, 126-131.*

For additional books, please contact the address below or contact the publisher of this book. May God bless and keep you in the months and years ahead.